The Best Laid Plans

Our Planning and Affordable Housing Challenges in Marin

By

Bob Silvestri

Cover Design: Bob Silvestri

Photos: Mill Valley, California

Copyright © 2012 Robert J. Silvestri;   All rights reserved.

ISBN: 978-1480144422

Cataloging Publication Data

1. Affordable Housing   2.Community   3. Marin 4. Planning

This book is dedicated to everyone who has worked to make government responsive to community voices.

*"The best laid schemes of Mice and Men
oft go awry,
And leave us nothing but grief and pain,
For promised joy!"*

~ Robert Burns - 1785

CONTENTS

ACKNOWLEDGMENTS

There are many people to thank for the experiences that led to writing this book. I suppose I should first thank all those "top down," regional planners, highly paid consultants and government officials, whose unrealistic ideas drove me to write it.

I want to thank my friends, Rob Dick and Maurice Bennett, for their unwavering belief in my work. And I want to thank many of our local community leaders, Susan Kirsch, Burton Miller, Liz Specht, David LaDuke and Mitch Wortzman, and those affiliated with Friends of Mill Valley, and so many others throughout Marin County, who have worked tirelessly for years to help bring about reasonable solutions to complex community problems.

I'd also like to thank Dana Curtin for helping me publish this book. And Tom Dicker and Dick Spotswood, whose support and encouragement inspired me to do it.

And finally, a shout out to someone who is wise beyond his twelve years of age and keeps me focused on the present, Jesse Keefe.

FOREWORD

By Dick Spotswood

The phenomenon of well-intended people determined to tell their fellow countrymen how to live their lives emerged at the beginning of the twentieth century. Before that epoch, most thought they were doing well if they could manage their own affairs.

The reaction of the British Victorians and their American counterparts to major changes to society was often a Protestant-motivated urge to step in and "do something." The precipitating factor in Britain and their dominions was the rise of industrialization and the movement of peasants from farms to crowded cities. In America, the motivation sprang both from the rural-to-urban influx mixed with the arrival of immigrants, usually Catholics from southern Europe and Jews from Eastern Europe, living in a manner that the old guard didn't approve of.

Reformers today still share an impulse to correct what they see as society's evils. Self righteous? Yes. Overconfident in their own qualities? True. Patronizing to those who they don't understand or like? Undoubtedly. Evil? No, they were and are the epitome of good intentions.

In this country, the reformers' instinct takes two forms. One good, one not so good.

The constructive strain is exemplified by those who enacted the Pure Food and Drug Act, ended child labor, and advocated for safer working conditions. This segment was less interested in social change than correcting what they saw as obvious abuses in business and government. On the public stage, Theodore Roosevelt was their herald.

The other side of the reform movement, often backing wide-spread social engineering, were those whose self-confidence knew no bounds. They always seemed to know what's right, were quick to judge and invariably were unaware or unconcerned about any unintended consequents that might result from their actions. Think Carrie Nation with her axe.

These early reformers didn't like what they saw and were determined to use the power of government to change the behavior of others. Their ultimate cause was Prohibition.

One group whose lifestyle appalled reformers were those just-off-the-boat immigrants that drank alcohol. Not the proper beverage of the farm, hard cider, but hard liquor consumed in urban, working class bars. For them, alcohol consumption represented an alien culture that would lead to no good. Their approach envisioned the abolition of alcohol as the solution to most of the evils they perceived in modern American life.

As a social experiment, the Eighteenth Amendment was a complete bust demonstrating the excesses of the reformers' instinct. Alcohol consumption actually increased, organized crime prospered and many Americans came to see their government as interfering in their lives for illegitimate reasons. To their utter frustration, the stubborn public refused to do what the reformers deemed best. While in hindsight these outcomes appear obvious, the reformers in their zeal were invariably blind to the prospects of what they unleashed.

Reformers by their nature possess a supreme self confidence that they, whether justified or not, always know better than others how to run things. It was and remains an instinct that sometimes leads to improved lives. Other times this impulse causes far more harm than it eradicates.

Occasionally, those pushing for what they see as reform are simply wrong. They lack the experience and perspective to understand whether every aspect of American life that they don't approve of should be changed. Restraint is a quality often missing from their makeup. Of course, if it turns out that their mission is wrongheaded, they comfort themselves that their intentions are pure. At worst, it's the lives of others that are on the line, not theirs.

Bob Silvestri's *The Best Laid Plans* thoughtfully chronicles when the reformers' instinct goes mad. He does so by detailing 21st century federal and state housing polices as executed by California regional planners.

The implementation of these government-mandated housing schemes, as carried out by indirectly-governed regional agencies, is a contemporary example of the lack of restraint and hubris emanating from those convinced that they always know what's best for others.

From his perspective in California's Marin County, Silvestri spots the problems caused by housing activists, big time developers and their allies in government. As a housing industry professional, Silvestri is sympathetic to aspects of the activists' agenda. This vantage provides him the ability to see the predictable but unintended consequences of their one-size-fits-all approach to planning and policy.

Are these activists and bureaucrats, who believe that America's most intractable problems can be solved simply by increasing the supply of housing, reformers of the positive or negative variety? Like modern prohibitionists, will they cause more harm than good? That's a call ultimately up to the reader.

What Bob Silvestri has done is neatly and readably outline what undoubtedly will happen to much of suburban America if these blunt and misguided efforts at social engineering go unchallenged.

The Best Laid Plans

PREFACE

This book began as a series of articles published in local newspapers. It was a reaction to what I perceived as a lack of courage on the part of our local political leaders to stand up to heavy-handed "social engineers" in Sacramento, determined to remake our cities in their own image.

My immediate goal was simply to start asking questions that needed to be asked. What were the problems we were really trying to solve? Were there alternatives to the monotonous, high density proposals regional planners were trying to cram down our throats? Certainly, there must be ways to preserve the good things about our small communities and still encourage diversity and social equity.

As I looked deeper, I realized that we needed new ways of thinking about the world, about concepts like "growth" and "progress." We needed to create a process to plan for a future that might surprise us and not be more of the same things we've known in the past. The public discussion was simply too narrow, locked into a "for" or "against" dynamic. Basic assumptions weren't being properly challenged. We were inundated with endless "studies" and experts and statistics but they always resulted in more of the same. And community voices weren't being given a proper seat at the decision making table.

Like most people, I was never very involved in local politics or city planning issues. I'd moved around a lot, was too busy with my career and my life, and generally rationalized my lack of interest for all the usual reasons. It's ironic because as an architect and an affordable housing developer, I'd worked with lots of city governments and planning departments. But that was "business." Besides, I'd grown up in New York City, where they teach you from birth that you "can't fight City Hall," so I was somewhat cynical about politics or politicians, anyway.

All this changed when I bought a home in Mill Valley, almost 20 years ago, a place where I'd dreamed of living since I graduated college.

Marin County is a magical place. Every year millions of people come from around the world to cross the Golden Gate Bridge to take picture perfect photos of the San Francisco skyline from the magnificent Marin Headlands, and explore our vast open spaces, sandy beaches, and charming small towns. Mill Valley is one of its crown jewels, nestled up against the foot of Mt. Tamalpais.

When I first arrived, I was just grateful to be able to live here. I was eager to expand the small (925 square foot) house I'd bought, to make it more livable, and was engrossed in getting to know the area. City planning was the furthest thing from my mind. But no sooner had I settled in than I found out that "the City," without bothering to consult a single homeowner in our neighborhood, had decided to "down-zone" our area. This meant that we would no longer be allowed to expand the size of our homes.

The powers that be had decided that in response to rising home prices, our neighborhood should forever be a place for small "starter homes" that would be relatively less expensive to buy. The fact that none of the City Council members actually lived in our neighborhood but instead lived in huge homes up in the canyons that would be free of such restrictions, seemed a bit unfair to me but didn't seem to bother them a bit. So I was forced to take action.

Working with my new neighbors, we quickly set up a system of block captains to canvas our area to spread the word and we circulated a petition against the proposal (no Change.org or Internet back then). Within weeks we'd gathered signatures from about 80 percent of the homeowners and brought our fight to the council chambers. Seeing this groundswell of angry opposition, the City backed down and has never brought it up since.

It was a sweet victory. But more importantly, it was good to know that our individual voices, working together, could bring about real change. But little did I know it was just the beginning.

Ten years later, our fair city hatched a massive scheme to completely transform the main business artery into town, Miller Avenue. The Miller Avenue Precise Plan, as it was called, proposed to turn a walkable, pleasantly scaled street (one and two story buildings), that was home to many locally owned, service businesses (auto repair, bike shops, food stores, clothing and antique stores, cafes and sandwich shops, yoga studios, dry cleaners, gas stations, etc.), into a three and four story, mixed use, "Smart Growth" vision of retailing and apartment living that only a highly paid consultant who didn't live here could love.

Once again, we were facing down a proposal that would be have negative impacts on our working class and middle class neighborhoods, but leave the more exclusive downtown and hillside neighborhoods untouched. And once again, it came wrapped in an "affordable housing" marketing campaign.

I consider myself an advocate for affordable housing opportunities for everyone. I used to make a living turning market rate properties into Section 8 affordable units that my partners and I owned and managed. But affordable housing or any housing for that matter has to be appropriate for its location. And to succeed, any plan has to be based on comprehensive community goals that are economically, socially and environmentally sustainable. Dropping an out-of-scale, urban, ideologically derived solution smack down in the middle of our sleepy little town was not going to cut it.

However, this time the City had brought more firepower to the table. They'd enlisted an entourage of high paid consultants to "educate" the community about the virtues of their plan. They held elaborate "public workshops" and "information sessions" that sounded great but in fact were tightly orchestrated PR gambits, crafted to make sure the outcomes were exactly as planned. Those who protested were labeled as "difficult" and their objections were dismissed. "Style" triumphed over substance and though the City made a great pretense of "listening" to all points of view, nothing but the desired message was "heard." This time we had a real problem on our hands.

One night in March of 2007, nine people met in a small conference room at a local bank to see how we might mobilize the community. It didn't take long. Within weeks we had an organization name, a mission statement, a logo, a newsletter and a tag line that guided us, "Let's do it right!"

Instead of just waiting for the city to change, we decided to do all the things the city wasn't doing. We conducted public opinion polls, created a "Community News" email sign up list, and held town halls to allow anyone to come and make their opinions known. And by November, when the elections for seats on the city council rolled around, our email list had reached over 1,000 registered voters (in a town where only 3,500 voters turned out on Election Day) and we had petitions in hand with an equal number of signers.

The Miller Avenue Plan never saw the light of day again. Over time, those few things that were good about it (continuous bicycle lanes, preserving the unique character of different sections of the street) were incorporated in our planning process, which was a good thing. And we learned a lot.

We learned that there are three fundamental pieces to a successful community activist campaign: First, make noise: protest, petition, and write letters, whatever it takes, because if you don't, no one will take you seriously. The powers that be will slander you, but they'll be forced to take notice. Second, create doubt. This involves the heavy lifting of analyzing the specifics of what you're opposed to and detailing its fatal flaws. It is hard work but no one else will do it if you don't. And third, propose solutions. As unfair as it is, sometimes the only way to get anything done is to do all the work the city should have done in the first place (without being paid the enormous fees the consultants got for doing it wrong), then give the city all the credit.

Politicians are not evil, but unfortunately, far too many are followers, not leaders. However, the good news is that once they identify where the "critical mass" is heading, or sense a tipping point in public opinion, most are usually quick to jump in front of that "parade." So make sure the parade is about what you want it to be about.

Our struggle for appropriate planning solutions in Mill Valley also proved something very important that the city has never forgotten. We proved that the most important component of good planning is authentic and robust community participation in the planning process. We felt vindicated, but what we didn't realize was how powerful the forces were behind the push to urbanize our beloved small town.

Today we face a bigger challenge. In the wake of the 2008 crash, California politicians and big finance and development interests have gone into hyper-mode in an attempt to bring back a booming, real estate driven economy that will never return. Their new stalking horse is "affordable housing." And they've wrapped it up in a "jobs" banner and justified it as necessary for the health of the environment. In the San Francisco Bay Area the Association of Bay Area Governments (ABAG) and the Metropolitan Transportation Commission (MTC) are leading the charge. They enforce "top down" planning directives, handed down by Sacramento politicians, demanding annual, state-mandated "housing quotas." Their carrot and stick are state transportation funds. Our cash-strapped little cities have few defenses against this pro-development juggernaut.

When I started writing about all this, I had no idea how people might react. I knew my fellow community activists supported it, but it turned out that my articles resonated with many people in cities and counties all over Marin and Sonoma and beyond. And now, finally, even some of our elected officials are joining in. Better late than never.

My guess is that what we're experiencing in Marin may be happening in many small cities all across the country. My hope is that this book will in some way add to the conversation that helps us develop truly sustainable and equitable planning and affordable housing solutions.

CHAPTER I

A Brief History of Planning

Pruitt Igoe Demolition – St. Louis, MO 1973 – HUD Archives

"Adriana, if you stay here though, and this becomes your present then pretty soon you'll start imagining another time was really your... you know, was really the golden time."

~ Midnight in Paris – Woody Allen

In the late 1800's, the social and economic disruptions caused by the Industrial Revolution sparked a back-to-nature movement (inspired by the writers like Thoreau) and utopian communities sprang up across the country. But others believed that industrialization would bring about another kind of utopia: one filled with scientific wonders and new opportunity for all. But the dawning of the 20th century brought surprises no one imagined.

The promise of the Industrial Revolution gave way to the financial panic of 1905 (when the federal government had to be bailed out by JP Morgan), the war to end all wars (WWI), the

Depression of 1921, the Roaring Twenties and finally the Crash of 1929. The ensuing Great Depression left the public shaken.

By 1933, life seemed like an unending litany of booms and busts and scandals. Distrust of big business and government was at an all-time high. The majority of wealth was controlled by a small percentage of the population and the disparity between rich and poor had reached historic proportions. And the political landscape had become increasingly polarized on the left and the right.

Meanwhile, the general public was suffering from the worst real estate crash in history and they just wanted someone to get people back to work. Until the crash, people had been living high on the hog but now that seemed gone forever. People were very angry and they wanted "change."

Sound familiar? History seems to be repeating itself, for better and for worse. But notwithstanding the years dedicated to fighting World War II, or ironically because of it, in the decades that followed taxes got raised, markets and finances were regulated, the middle class thrived, and the American century came into its own.

A Very Brief History of City Planning

City planning has been with us forever. Alexandria, Athens, Rome, Tikal, Paris and Washington, D.C., were all carefully planned, albeit from the very top down. It's even claimed that the reason Nero fiddled while Rome burned was because he wanted to do major urban renewal and starting from scratch was the best way to eliminate "community opposition."

But the planning of our towns and cities (rather than seats of government) got a major boost from the challenges of the early 20th century when a new idea was born.

From Bauhaus to Your House

There's something about human nature that gravitates toward big, simplistic solutions when faced with complex problems. And faced with the multitude of wocs in the 1930's, many believed that massive housing projects were the way to solve our social and economic problems.

This view was shared by many social reformers and prominent architects and planners of the time, who proceeded to take a plausible idea and completely overdo it. "Modern" architecture and planning, as it came to be known, embraced mass production and technological innovation and promised to create cities that showcased the wonders of the Industrial Age. This egalitarian and utilitarian ideal, proselytized by Walter Gropius and the German Bauhaus, was perhaps most famously expressed by an obscure painter turned architect named Charles-Édouard Jeanneret (who changed his name to Le Corbusier - perhaps being the first artist to take on a one name moniker).

The Radiant City

For "Modernists" like Corbusier, housing people was an industrial undertaking and humanity's needs were utilitarian (fresh air, sunlight, sanitation, human scaled space, clean water and a view). This culminated in a vision he called *La Ville Radieuse* (The Radiant City).

The Radiant City envisioned thousands of boxy, well lit, unadorned living units stacked in towering glass, concrete and steel skyscrapers built in close proximity to transportation (automotive super highways) and within walking distance to shopping and other necessities ("The more things change…").

Unfortunately, grand visions tend to be doomed to grand failures.

To be fair, the modernists were as much driven by concern about public health conditions for the 99 percent as they were by trying to house the masses: there was little fresh air or natural light and few private bathrooms in 19th century tenements and housing conditions for the masses in general were abysmal. The times called for bold action and optimism about grandiose solutions. Our innate love of all things new and shiny proved irresistible.

So when our federal government looked for ways to solve the demand for new housing in the 1940's after WWII, they looked to Modernists' visions.

Projects like Stuyvesant Town / Peter Cooper Village in New York City, built in 1947, housed almost 100,000 people in one high density location (the Radiant City in Manhattan). And the demand for housing at that time, after decades of almost no housing construction, was very real.

Proponents claimed it had everything required to ensure its success. It was a "walkable," modern village close to schools, shopping and public transportation. But what began in the late 40's as a vision of equality and affordable housing opportunity became a dystopian nightmare, unflatteringly known as the "projects" by the 1960's.

To have grown up in the projects was synonymous with having had a deprived, crime-filled childhood that you dreamed of escaping. Somehow "warehousing" people near public transportation and in walking distance from shopping just didn't magically bring about equality, harmony or happiness.

Perhaps I'm just spit-balling here, but maybe it had something to do with the complete lack of opportunity for individual expression and other less tangible human needs.

By the early 1970's, these massive experiments in social engineering had clearly failed and we began tearing down high density affordable housing projects across the country. Pruitt Igoe in St. Louis (2,870 units) was the most infamous but by no means the only example. Yet somehow this lesson continues to escape the "one size fits all" central planners today.

New Urbanism

By the 1980's and early 1990's, it became obvious that we needed a new take on things. Fiscal conservatism became the new fashion and federal funds for housing were drying up faster than the Sacramento River Delta. Consequently, city planning became more about urban renewal, historic preservation and zoning codes than about building cities of the future.

Left in a lurch, planners swung 180 degrees in the other direction and embraced the back-to-nature utopian ideals of the last century, but this time with a new twist. This was a new kind of nostalgia for the past that came wrapped in a new phrase: "sustainable living."

Seaside, Florida. *The Truman Show*

It was called "New Urbanism."

Towns would now instantly have all the "character" of small town Americana. New Urbanism preached the benefits of walkable communities near shopping, amenities and public transportation. It was based on observing successful small towns and attempted to reproduce the lifestyle they enjoyed. The only problem is there's a lot more to what creates "community" than meets the eye.

New Urbanism envisioned winding streets lined with quaint Craftsman-like clapboard homes on small lots, with people chatting with neighbors from rocking chairs on wooden porches behind white picket fences. Neighborhoods were laid out around quaint "town squares" with housing districts separated from commercial areas by green space. In many ways these plans were almost an exact copy of the utopian towns that were designed and built in the U.S. from the late 1800's and the early 1900's.

There's no argument that there are compelling reasons for living in a more humanized environment. Just ask anyone who lives in Marin County. But at the end of the day, the New Urbanism vision is superficial and its "community" is as faux as the shiplap siding on its cutesy bungalows.

New Urbanism is like Ralph Lauren was in the 1980's. Both try to sell us a nostalgic, patina-tinged vision of a past that never actually existed. Rather than doing the hard work of rethinking our world from the bottom up, addressing inter-related socio-economic realities and offering a truly new vision of our future potential, New Urbanism offers us a sentimental throwback to a Norman Rockwell painting belief about who we are. But in the face of our 21st century challenges, it's devoid of sustainable answers because we are not those imaginary people and we don't live those imaginary lives.

New Urbanism planners have made their careers out of selling a vision of simpler times to a world-weary public. But in reality, the promises of New Urbanism are empty.

Interestingly, New Urbanism was originally conceived to improve upon and make some sense out of suburban sprawl. It is actually mislabeled. It should be called "suburban-renewal." It primarily focused on better ways to build single family housing in places completely devoid of character (examples include, Laguna West near Sacramento, Denver Stapleton Airport Redevelopment, or Seaside, Florida, which was used in the motion picture, *The Truman Show*, because of its "too perfect" small town look).

These were perfectly legitimate goals. But New Urbanism wanted to get people out of cars mostly to enhance social interaction and small town character, not because of presumptuous claims about mitigating climate change. Likewise, New Urbanism was not originally about affordable housing. But in an attempt to remain relevant, it has been turned to the dark side.

Planners like Peter Calthorpe now work for major suburban developers like Forest City Enterprises, and New Urbanism and its oxymoronic step-child "Smart Growth" have become synonymous with social engineering by big government agencies promoting infill, high density housing near freeways and over-reaching control of local zoning to try to recapture a quaint, long-gone world where shopkeepers lived in tiny apartments over their stores (an obsolete model that has been replaced in the 21st century by live/work lofts for telecommuters and business incubators, office sharing hubs for budding entrepreneurs).

This unfortunate fusion of top down control has given us what might be described as the worst of both dystopian worlds: the faux "sustainable" community of the "back to simpler times" movement combined with the high density near transportation / housing for the masses visions of the Modernists. And in the middle, real communities like our small towns in Marin, which were built on decades of local control and environmental protection, are being thrown under the bus in the name of progress.

The results are projects like the 180-unit WinCup development, located next to the 101 highway off ramps in Corte Madera, and the Millworks mixed use project in Novato (Whole Foods and condos). Building projects like this as "infill" won't make them work any better than their larger scaled predecessors. It's a sure bet that in 20 years these will not be among the most desirable places to live.

Perhaps the most absurd irony of all though is that we now have Peter Calthorpe coming to Marin to preach to us about the virtues of New Urbanism, when in fact it is towns like ours that were the inspiration for New Urbanism in the first place.

I think our citizens know better than anyone what "community" and "walkable neighborhoods" and "small town character" are. The New Urbanism planners of the world should be coming to Marin to learn not to preach. We don't need their definition of "sustainable" but they sure do need ours. Yet we find ourselves having to fight against the New Urbanist / Smart Growth mantra to preserve what we have: the very thing they profess to want to create. Figure that one out.

In truth, New Urbanism's solutions are not really more sustainable. Their greenhouse gas (GHG) emissions savings are nonexistent. Their building methods are conventional and just as environmentally destructive as anything else. And implementing its concepts without first addressing the underlying social and economic causes of social inequity is fiscally irresponsible.

Who's not for a Sustainable Future?

Let's face it. Everyone is for "sustainable solutions." But those solutions need to actually be socially, economically and environmentally sustainable after considering their true costs of "natural capital" and their external affects (supply chain energy usage, third world environmental degradation, etc.; see *Natural Capitalism* by Paul Hawken). New Urbanism and the "One Bay Area" approach are not that.

The *One Bay Area Plan* is a regional planning concept being heavily promoted in Marin by the Association of Bay Area Governments (ABAG) and the Metropolitan Transportation Commission (MTC).

ABAG is a regional, quasi-governmental, super agency that sprang from humble beginnings to become a major force in local planning, land use, housing, environmental quality, and economic development. Begun in 1961 as a way for communities to coordinate their efforts for the common good, ABAG is now the errand boy for major financial interests and social engineers in Sacramento. They administer a housing "quota" system (based on the State's Regional Housing Needs Allocation assessment - RHNA) that's passed down by the Department of Housing and Community Development with dictatorial fervor.

MTC, created in 1970 for the purposes of coordinating transportation services in the nine county Bay Area, has likewise morphed into a mega-agency, doling out grants and transportation dollars to those willing to swallow its social engineering agenda.

Working together, their *One Bay Area Plan* proposes planning solutions that would turn our unique small towns into homogenized, Smart Growth, "urban" centers.

These two quasi-public agencies, with no real public accountability, are increasingly attempting to usurp local control of planning and land use in the name of better planning coordination and affordable housing demand. But their planning methods and development assumptions are just more of the same old thing we've been doing for fifty years. They look at the future as if it will only be more of what we've had in the past rather than considering the potential impacts of social, economic and technological change that is clearly coming. But what they fail to understand is that the nature of growth and development is not just about "building." In short, they lack "vision."

What we really need are solutions that are truly environmentally sustainable *and* address our social equity challenges at the same time. We need solutions that make fiscal sense for our cities and financial sense to private capital markets.

That is the problem before us. But instead we find ourselves faced with an unappetizing menu of "high density" options and massive bureaucracies trying to force one size fits all solutions down our throats, none of which are sustainable in any real sense of the word.

But there was another idea that came out of the 1930's that was totally ignored in its day and has been derided by historians ever since. Its author was not a popular man. He was the quintessential "politically incorrect" designer of his time. But it was the only vision that actually addressed long term sustainability. Maybe there are things we can learn from it.

Photo Credits:

The Radiant City – Wikipedia Foundation
Stuyvesant Town / Peter Cooper Village – Wikipedia Foundation
Seaside, Florida – Wikipedia Foundation

CHAPTER II

21st Century Planning

Broadacre City, 1935 – Frank Lloyd Wright Foundation

"The Internet is based on a layered, end-to-end model that allows people at each level of the network to innovate free of any central control. By placing intelligence at the edges rather than control in the middle of the network, the Internet has created a platform for innovation."   ~ Vint Cerf

When you develop Internet software, the only thing you can be sure of is that everything you're sure of will probably change because innovation is happening everywhere in the long tail. It is the ultimate "bottom up" system. This means that designing for it requires solutions that embrace user interactivity, open-ended design, flexibility, and methods that "learn" and adapt to change. I think city planning can be that way. In fact I think it will have to be because whether we like it or not, the coming century will be an increasingly bottom up, networked, borderless, telecommuting, personally expressive, crowd-sourced world.

I know. It sounds like a lot of big words. But think about it. We need alternative approaches to the planning methods we employ today. We need methods that are more responsive and adaptable to the nuances of local public policy needs and the ever-changing dynamics of private capital markets. Methods that highlight the importance of enabling individual initiative and local empowerment in solving planning problems. But where will these new ideas come from?

In Chapter IV, I propose using a new "criteria-based" planning method to achieve these objectives. However, my inspiration came from that third planning vision that came out of the 1930's.

The Bad Boy of Planning

Frank Lloyd Wright was perhaps the most controversial architect in modern history. His iconoclastic career was unique even among American visionaries. Always the rebel, he never bothered to get a license to practice until he was in his 70's, by which time he'd designed or built more than 600 buildings. By today's standards he'd be called a Libertarian. (Note: the Marin County Civic Center was Wright's last commission before his death.)

Wright absolutely hated top down planning and big government. He'd be rolling over in his grave if he knew about ABAG and the *One Bay Area Plan*. When it came to city planning, Wright was a staunch advocate of "local control."

Wright called his planning vision Broadacre City. Like the other planning concepts of the Depression Era, its goals were to enhance the fortunes of the common man by creating a more egalitarian society. But after that it diverged completely from the orthodoxy of Modern urbanism because it wasn't urban at all.

Universally dismissed by critics of the time, it turned out to be the most durable idea of all because it foresaw the rise of suburbia. In fact it has been blamed for all the ills of suburbia but that's just because Broadacre City's concept was never fully understood or appreciated.

Unlike the Modernist's high-density, glass and concrete cities or utopianism's back to nature schemes, Broadacre City might be called the "40 acres and a mule" school of planning. Wright aimed for a balance between nature and man's footprint on the planet. He was a strong proponent of individual creativity and personal self-sufficiency long before it was fashionably called "sustainable."

Wright envisioned an adaptive plan wherein every family had its own sustainable one acre plot, large enough to grow some food, capture rainwater, have a windmill and raise a few animals. He envisioned "growth" as an organic process that was mostly horizontal, with occasional instances of high rise development (his famous "mile-high" skyscraper design being an example of that).

Now there's no doubt that Wright's ideas were in some ways even more fanciful than the other planning visions of his time. But Wright was essentially talking about living "off the grid" or at least not being dominated by it. Like the way the Internet is managed today, he was talking about planning that had no central control point but was designed and developed by local users for local conditions "at the edges," all within a flexible framework that optimized outcomes for all.

In this respect, he was way ahead of his time.

Technology and Sustainability

California Senate Bill 375 (SB375) was signed into law in September of 2008, a month before the onset of the housing mortgage banking debacle. It was a law driven by big builder and big banking interests with an insatiable appetite for more and more development and profits, in a state where entitled land was growing scarce. Its superficial premise was that building high density housing near public transportation would reduce greenhouse gas emissions (GHGs).

Unfortunately, SB375's assumptions are deeply flawed.

I'll go into this in greater detail in Chapter V, but suffice it to say that SB375 and the *One Bay Area Plan* approach would have us believe that we have to accept the Modernist / New Urbanism high density near public transportation vision of the future. It's a rigid and single-minded view in which suburban living is singled out as the major problem. But it's not based on facts.

The greenhouse gas (GHG) emissions savings assumptions of SB375 and its progeny, the *One Bay Area Plan*, incorrectly assume that the things we make (our vehicles, buildings, appliances, etc.) are immutable givens that will never change. But there's no evidence that this is true or is even likely to be true in the future.

Furthermore, the vertical, high-density cities it envisions are not actually, in and of themselves, a sustainable solution.

Cities are an "economic" solution and perhaps a "social" solution. But today our biggest cities are, on an overall basis *and a per capita basis*, the most egregious polluters on the planet, not just in terms of GHG emissions but also when one accounts for all the impacts on surrounding regions to "feed" them with water and power and deal with their waste.

In fact the number one "user" of energy in its creation and on an everyday basis is "buildings." Our homes, commercial offices, institutional, industrial, etc. represent 40 percent of our total ongoing energy usage and their construction is *the most resource intensive endeavor on the planet* with supply chain impacts that add huge multiples to energy use and socio-economic / environmental impacts worldwide.

Cars and Trucks

Robert Lutz, the famous automotive pioneer and former head of General Motors, recently said that within 10 years battery technology will have reached a point where the internal combustion engine will no longer be able to compete economically with electric powered vehicles and will become obsolete with or without legislation: this coming from the man who invented the "muscle car" in the 1960's.

It's obvious that GHG emissions and pollution from automobiles, along with vehicle technology, not only can change but are changing dramatically as we speak (e.g. the new 2013 Ford C-Max Energi, plug-in hybrid will get more than 100 miles per gallon).

If our cars and trucks begin to average about 40 mpg (this technology, hybrid or electric, is readily available today) and more importantly, regardless of engine type, they meet ZEV standards (Zero Emissions Vehicle – many hybrids already do this), the car will no longer an important GHG contributor. So why in the world would we base an enormously disruptive and expensive long-term plan on the premise that it is?

Concepts like the *One Bay Area Plan* are pushing us to build many times the amount of housing we actually need to meet historical growth rates. All this housing will be constructed using traditional, high GHG producing building methods because truly "green" building technologies are not yet commonly or economically available. This will only add to our climate change challenges.

So with all this considered, shouldn't we be planning for the future instead of the past?

The ability to produce zero pollution and super energy-efficient vehicles, buildings and mechanical equipment is within our reach. It only requires national, state and local public policy to make it happen (just as agri-business and oil and gas subsidies make those things happen). But there is another "elephant in the room" that is not even acknowledged by the One Bay Area approach, though it may be even more important than all the rest.

Power, Water and Waste Systems

Achieving a sustainable future and planning for change also includes how we distribute power and water and collect and process waste. Throughout history the need to share and efficiently distribute resources from a central location (e.g. water from a river or natural spring) has been a given. This is so ingrained in our thinking that we accept it without questioning its long term sustainability challenges. But by all measures centralized utility systems are incredibly wasteful and inefficient. This gets even worse in suburbia where the distances between users and the sources of power or water or the distance to sewage treatment plants is greater.

Significant losses occur as electrical power moves out through our vast centralized power grids. A large percentage of our drinking water is lost due to leakage and evaporation as it moves through underground pipes and aqueducts. And in many U.S. metropolitan areas, 50 percent of the effluent that goes into sewer lines never reaches the treatment plant because it leaches out into the ground through old pipes. And then there's the cost of building and maintaining these centralized systems and the support services, which create even more pollution and waste.

When it comes to really addressing our environmental challenges and the host of options at hand, all this becomes very important to consider because efficient use of resources is fundamental to any environmentally or economically sustainable solution. So we have to ask ourselves, is there a better way? And if there is, what model should we be looking to for guidance?

The Nature of Nature

The history of the world is the history of going from simplicity to diversity, from single-celled organisms to multi-celled marvels, and from isolated linear systems to complex inter-related networks and "systems of systems." Throughout that process, nature's problem-solving methods have favored bottom up and locally driven solutions that allow for the nuances and constraints of local conditions. But there are more benefits to nature's way than respecting local control and encouraging diversity.

Nature's top-to-bottom and bottom-to-top interactive feedback methods tend to result in solutions that are the most energy, time and resource efficient possible for all participants. Because of real-time interactivity between local and global, nature's methods are constantly optimizing outcomes for all.

Consider three examples: the way your brain is wired, how a vine grows on a fence and the infrastructure of the Internet.

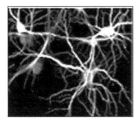  

Each is elegantly adapted to solve "local" problems in a way that addresses specific needs, and at the same time allow the entire networked "organism" to operate as efficiently as possible without central control. This is the secret of their success.

21st Century Interactive Planning

City planning has followed the same trajectory as nature, evolving from enclosed city states into networks of cities separated by vast expanses, until the edges of cities expanded to the point where everything got connected and we have the megalopolis we live in today: networks of inter-related entities with both shared concerns and unique problems. But we're at a tipping point in history. The top-down, centrally controlled state and regional planning methods that made sense in the past are now too rigid and unresponsive to address the complexity of our contemporary world.

Looking ahead, what we need are methods that enhance greater interaction between the top and the bottom, maximize local input and local control of planning decisions, and encourage diverse and novel solutions. The implications of this for our political process, legal framework and planning hierarchies are enormous. Interactivity even suggests the need for our representative form of government to finally transform into a "one person, one vote" true democracy.

This brings us back to Frank Lloyd Wright. It's important to recognize that the fundamental limitations of Wright's sustainable concepts were technological. The technology required to make his ideas feasible simply didn't exist. However, today we have the ability to realize Wright's self-sufficiency and environmental / community / sustainability goals.

In the near future every vehicle we produce will be pollution free and run on sustainable power (electricity, hydrogen fuel cells, biofuels, etc.), and every building could be carbon neutral and produce most of its own power. And buildings could harvest and recycle gray water and treat much of their waste on site.

Consider the following:

Water:

Water conserving appliances and equipment, drip irrigation, rainwater capture and gray water recycling can dramatically reduce the amount of water needed and force us to rethink our water distribution methods. This is already happening enough to put the Marin

Municipal Water District's business model in jeopardy because the more users conserve, the more MMWD has to charge them for water.

Waste:

"Closed-loop" waste technology that separates and treats waste on site has been around for more than 40 years. It's time that this was given more careful consideration. These systems can greatly reduce the need to expand or upgrade sewer systems and can increase the opportunities to produce recycled waste products.

Recycling and banning plastic bags is just the tip of the iceberg of the change that is possible when it comes to dealing with our trash.

Energy:

Advances in energy-conserving products and alternative energy sources are about to tip the balance of global energy production and distribution from the top to the bottom. Feeding power in one direction out to users on the grid, from central power plants (i.e. hydroelectric plants, nuclear reactors, coal fired generators, etc.) is technologically obsolete. "Smart Grids" distribute power the way the Internet distributes information and dramatically alter the "user / producer" relationship.

Interactive, self-monitoring electrical grids change a "distribution" network into a "sharing" network where everyone becomes both a user and a producer. New thin-film photovoltaics can produce solar energy on any surface (even window glass). Wind is the fastest growing new energy source in the world and residential, rooftop wind generators should start showing up at Home Depot within the next decade. More options will be here sooner than people think, especially if we encourage them.

As Amory Lovins has so famously said, it's all about "reduce, reuse, recycle." Every product we manufacture needs to address its energy consumption and waste output not just during its use but during its entire lifecycle, from natural resource extraction through production to recycling. This is true for the buildings we build, the vehicles we drive, the food we grow, and the gadgets we consume with abandon. It's called "Cradle to Cradle" design. [1]

Even things like urban farming are transforming our cities and demonstrating the efficiencies of solving "demand" problems at the source.

But again, this won't happen without public will and public policy to support it. So if our government is going to provide financial incentives for anything, perhaps this is money better spent than the hundreds of billions we spend annually subsidizing military arms, oil and coal, sugar and corn.

What Does This Have To Do With Planning?

All this suggests that future growth may be much more about renovation, reuse, conservation and technologically retrofitting what we already have (like putting rooftop solar on every building) than about "scrape and build" construction and the grandiose planning methods that dominated the 20th century. This is not science fiction. These are the things we have to do if we ever hope to offer the next generation a reasonable future. And if even half of what I'm suggesting comes to pass, it will have profound implications for the future of planning.

If adaptive technology can re-engineer our lives and automobiles will no longer pollute or rely on fossil fuels, then all the "urban" versus "suburban" arguments fall apart. In fact lower density suburban solutions may have significant environmental and quality of life advantages over high density urban solutions. At the very least, there's room for a wide variety of locally driven solutions, all of which might be equally sustainable and all of which should be on the table for consideration instead of the one-sided thinking we're being force-fed by state and regional agencies like ABAG, MTC, Bay Conservation and Development Commission (BCBD), Bay Area Air Quality Management District (BAAQMD) and others.

Solving Problems at the Source

I live in a 1,830-square-foot house on a 50 by 125 ft. lot. I have landscaped yards with six kinds of fruit trees and a sizeable vegetable garden, all fed by automated drip irrigation. I compost most organic waste and produce very little trash. I drive a hybrid car. My appliances and fixtures are energy saving and low flow. My electric bill averages less than $90 per month. For almost that same monthly cost, on a leased basis, I'm considering installing solar panels which would provide 100 percent of my electrical needs now and when I purchase a plug-in electric car in the future. If I had a rainwater capture and gray water waste recycling system, I'd pretty much be off the grid, or in the case of electricity, selling back to the grid.

Someone please explain to me how this is not a sustainable solution. Someone please explain to me why we're not creating every incentive we can to allow everyone to renovate and retrofit their homes to live this way, or why all new residential (single family and multifamily) and commercial buildings shouldn't be designed to have far less environmental impact

(Leadership in Energy and Environmental Design Standards (LEED) are not enough).

Public policy supporting this would create thousands of new businesses and tens of millions of 21st century hi-tech jobs across the country versus short term, low pay construction and service jobs that come and go.

Why is it we're not hearing anything about these options from ABAG / MTC and our elected officials? Have we really become that unimaginative or that pessimistic about our future? How can we expect anything to change if we don't bring about change right here in our own communities? Do we really want to bet our future on the dismal, over-reaching plans of engorged government agencies?

The arguments that "urban" is good and "suburban" is bad, or "high density" is superior to "low density" are off base. Our path to a better future is through solving problems in the most efficient and mutually beneficial way possible. And I believe that it's the right combination of financial backstop from the top and locally driven public policy and decision making at the bottom that can best ensure that outcome.

Looking Ahead

Myopic high-density scenarios like the *One Bay Area Plan* are out of synch with the multi-faceted way the future of our cities and infrastructure is likely to unfold. It deals in fixed absolutes and views things from only one direction: producers to users, and sellers to buyers. Jobs and workers are just numbers devoid of human proclivities and choice. It fails to account for our increasingly interactive world and how creative private capital and public policy changes can dramatically affect predictions based on the status quo.

This is particularly critical right now because we don't have the luxury of unlimited resources or unlimited wealth to squander on bad ideas. The faulty assumptions of laws like SB375 will lead to more bad decisions and more misallocation of taxpayer money. And applying its faulty logic to other challenges, like affordable housing, has already led to even more damaging ideas such as California Senate Bill 1220 (SB1220) that proposes to levy additional local taxes to create a massive billion dollar slush fund in Sacramento to fund affordable housing development, without any local control or public oversight, or Senate Bill 226 (SB226) that proposes to eliminate California Environmental Quality Act review (CEQA) for "infill" projects, thereby undermining the very thing SB375 pretends to be trying to preserve, our environment.

And finally there's the latest proposal by ABAG and MTC to pass a law that requires every Bay Area resident to install a GPS tracking device in their car so their movements can be monitored 24/7 by big government in order to charge them a tax of 10 cents per mile for every mile they drive, the proceeds of which would go into a black hole called the general fund of the Metropolitan Transportation Commission. And they are proposing this with a straight face contending that it will be good for the environment.

This is a road we cannot afford to go down.

Over-reaching top-down social engineering has failed us in the past and it will fail us again. Its approach is economically destabilizing and financially irresponsible because it contradicts the laws of supply and demand, free markets, and the way communities naturally grow and thrive. And it's ultimately environmentally destructive. And for what, more and more profits for big developers and big banking and financial interests?

But if all that's true, then how do we address our legitimate social justice and affordable housing concerns? And what about the portion of our population that is truly in great need, the people we really should be focusing on who are just getting by and need a helping hand or a "safety net" right now?

To answer these questions we need to know a bit more about how we got to where we are today.

Photo Credits:

Broadacre City – Frank Lloyd Wright Foundation
Brain Synapse – Scientific American
Vine on Fence – Public Domain
Internet Layout – Public Domain

Footnote:

[1] Cradle to Cradle, William McDonough and Michael Braungart; North Point Press, 2002

CHAPTER III

Affordable Housing

Dexter Asylum (Poor House), Providence RI 1824
Library of Congress

"Those who cannot remember the past are condemned to repeat it."
~ George Santayana

When I was growing up in New York City, where my family owned a small business, my father told me that the scariest words in the English language were, "We're from the government and we're here to help you." A lot of people feel that way about ABAG housing quotas and affordable housing projects in general. But it's more complicated than that.

Reasonable people might agree that having a variety of housing opportunities for those most in need, without discrimination, is a worthy societal goal. But there's a difference between "providing housing opportunities" and "building affordable housing." And affordable housing means different things to different people in different places. It includes homeless shelters, starter homes, rental apartments and townhouses, live/work lofts, SRO (single room occupancy) housing, elderly housing and assisted living, housing for very low and low income (below 30 percent to 50 percent median) and 80 percent median income "affordable" units like the ones we see being built all over Marin (for a family in Mill Valley earning about $90,000 per year).

So where should we focus our efforts and how do we define and prioritize our needs? Some history of how we got here helps.

A Brief History of Affordable Housing

Affordable housing in the U.S. was traditionally left to private markets or corporations that built "company towns" for their workers (e.g. Pullman, Illinois and Scotia, California). But the idea that the government should get directly involved (other than operating "poor houses" for the destitute) didn't really come into being until the Great Depression.

In 1934, the National Housing Act created the Federal Housing Administration (FHA) to help people protect their homes from foreclosure. The 1937 Housing Act, which coined the phrase "affordable housing," subsidized the construction of government-owned rental housing for the general public under Section 8 of the Act. After that the federal government quickly became the primary driver of affordable housing finance and construction.

The mid 1940's through the early 1960's was the Golden Age of government housing. The 1949 Housing Act and urban renewal legislation caused a building boom across the country to feed post World War II demand. Projects like Stuyvesant

Town / Peter Cooper Village in New York City, built by a "public–private partnership" in 1947, housed almost 100,000 people in one location.

The Winds of Change

The 1960's saw the passage of Fair Housing laws to ensure equal access to housing, an important advancement. But in the aftermath of the Vietnam War the nation turned more conservative. The costs of the war and Johnson's Great Society had been enormous. One of Richard Nixon's first actions as president in 1970 was to cut federal housing programs dramatically. The thinking was that we were sinking too deeply into debt and could no longer afford them.

To remedy some of the financial shortfalls that resulted, the Community Development Block Grants program was created in 1974 and modifications were made to Section 8 housing programs to allow low income renters to live in privately owned buildings. Signed into law by Gerald Ford, these changes also eliminated a good number of government-built public housing programs so construction started shifting back to the private sector. These were the first substantive changes since the 1930's. But the real turning point came when Ronald Reagan was elected in 1980. This marked the beginning of the end of the central role of the U.S. Department of Housing and Urban Development (HUD) in providing affordable housing, and the beginning of the "markets can solve everything" mantra.

The End of Federal Housing Programs

One of Reagan's stated goals was to get the federal government out of the housing business completely, and so the systematic dismantling of affordable housing support systems began in earnest.

In 1983, a Reagan-appointed commission recommended an end to all project-based Section 8 subsidies, except in the case of rehabilitation. They recommended that all subsidy programs shift from directly financing housing projects to giving individuals housing vouchers, in order to give private developers incentive to build affordable housing (vouchers are a rental payment coupon that a renter can use to live anywhere).

No new government-owned housing projects were approved for construction after Reagan's election.

Jack Kemp, a self-described "bleeding heart conservative," was arguably one of the most important architects of HUD's recent history. He became Secretary of HUD in 1989. Prior to that, he worked behind the scenes to help the Reagan Administration "privatize" the affordable housing business.

Government Co-insurance, wherein private banks took over the role of financing projects in exchange for government guarantees of their debt, became widely used. Housing "project revenue bonds" and leverage debt became fashionable methods to finance private development without personal risk. And newly created Low Income Tax Credits attracted investment banking, mutual fund and corporate money to fund projects that had federal Housing Assistance Payments (HAP) contracts in place to guarantee high rents and revenues.

This all worked great for a while until unscrupulous underwriting practices and too much leveraged debt brought on the Savings & Loan Crisis in the 1980's (which we have to thank for coining the phrase "too big to fail"). When it was over, multifamily development was stalled for years and the banking fiasco became another excuse to get rid of government housing programs, altogether.

The Knock-Out Punch

In the final coup de grace, the Office of Independent Council launched a massive investigation into "political influence peddling" at HUD in 1988. The investigation was based on the "shocking" revelation that subsidy grant decisions in Washington might be influenced by political favoritism and high paid lobbyists (OMG, there's "gambling at Rick's").

This seems quaint today and it had little to do with rooting out corruption. Secretaries went to jail while high rollers walked away scot free. And federal affordable housing programs never recovered.

Project-based subsidies (projects with HAP contracts) were greatly reduced. Co-insurance and renovation programs like the Moderate Rehabilitation program were scuttled. And all that was left were Section 8 vouchers and tentative annual allocations of Low Income Tax Credits that almost exclusively went to big nonprofit developers who resold them to major corporations and investment funds. But as bad as all this was, it was only the beginning.

Call 'em NIMBYs

In 1991, HUD issued a report entitled, *"Not in My Back Yard – The Advisory Commission on Regulatory Barriers to Affordable Housing."* Authored by Jack Kemp and signed by George Bush, Sr., it came to be known as the "NIMBY

REPORT." The NIMBY Report alleged that local planning and zoning control was an impediment to affordable housing development and had to be challenged.

But we have to ask ourselves, why would neo-con Republican politicians propose such a liberal Democratic-sounding idea? Was it because of genuine concern for the needy? Having personally had a front row seat to watch the goings on at HUD in Washington, D.C. at the time, I can say with confidence that it wasn't. To bring the neo-con ideological motives into relief, we need only swap the terms "affordable housing development" with "developer profits" and it becomes clear what the elimination of impediments was all about.

By the early 1990's, it was obvious that vouchers, Jack Kemp's pet program, had failed to increase the affordable housing supply as promised (without direct government subsidy contracts, projects no longer "penciled," financially speaking). And as the market weakness of the early 1990's gave way to a new building boom, developers needed more entitled land, and fast. As a result, the NIMBY Report, a pro-markets, pro-private developer profits, and pro-big banking campaign thinly camouflaged as an affordable housing policy, has been the rallying cry of ABAG, MTC and affordable housing advocates ever since.

It's ironic that liberal-minded, left-leaning social reformers, like the Marin Community Foundation, are advancing the NIMBY argument today, apparently oblivious to its origins or how it benefits the very things that they are trying to correct: a system based on profits and private gain over community values.

The NIMBY pro-development agenda formed the philosophical basis for the kinds of "straw man" arguments we're dealing with today. Resistance to any affordable housing project in Marin, no matter how ill-conceived that project may be, is immediately labeled as NIMBYism. But perhaps the resistance to affordable housing in Marin is less about NIMBYism than it is about the increasing loss of local control and community choice in how our communities grow and cope financially, and how to maintain our quality of life.

Ownership Will Save Us?

In 1994, the Government Accounting Office continued the assault on federally funded housing programs with a report that damned HUD for its wastefulness (never mind that HUD's total budget was a mere fraction of the U.S. budgets for defense, farm subsidy, oil subsidy, or other heavily lobbied line items). Subsequently, a bill was introduced in the House of Representatives in 1995 to permanently shut HUD down. It almost passed. Then in 1997, Congress removed the last linchpin of affordable housing law passed in 1937 that required the federal government to replace every affordable unit it tore down or put out of use.

From the mid-1990's onward, the affordable housing business remained a shadow of its former self. The new focus was home ownership, not rentals, probably because in a "more debt / more leverage" financial system driven by the lure of lucrative underwriting fees, the mortgage brokers, banks and investment bankers could "game" that system more profitably than the rental housing business (many multifamily funding loopholes were closed after the S&L crisis).

Then in 2003 Congress passed the *"American Dream Down Payment Initiative"* and the already inflating housing bubble started to expand more rapidly, and affordability went out the window. We became focused on the wonders of price appreciation as the solution to all our social equity problems.

We all know how that turned out.

Bubble-nomics

By 2007, it's estimated that more than 40 percent of new jobs being created annually in California were real estate related (finance, banking, mortgage underwriting, construction, materials, real estate sales, household furnishings, appliances, supporting services, gardeners, house cleaning and everything they sell at Home Depot). With stiff environmental regulations dating back to the 1970s standing in their way and housing demand skyrocketing, real estate development interests continued to worry about land scarcity and lengthy entitlement processes. They needed to "feed the beast." [1]

The California State Legislature came to their rescue and has been coming to their rescue ever since.

"Affordable housing" green-washed with climate change "concerns" was the perfect argument to defeat opposition and look like heroes doing it. Following the passage of state Assembly Bill 32 (AB32), which linked public transportation and high density housing with "environmental benefits," and fueled by the financial backing of moneyed special interest groups, Senator Darrell Steinberg [2] crafted SB375. SB375 capitalized on the "NIMBY" argument and added climate change as a new reason to usurp local zoning control, even though its claims of greenhouse gas emissions reductions were unsubstantiated. With the last obstacles to development swept away it looked like clear sailing into an endless building boom.

The 2008 crash changed everything.

The unsustainable levels of public and private debt that fueled the boom brought on the worst financial crisis in more than 50 years. Cities that over-extended themselves by building more and more housing ended up broke and may never fully recover (Vallejo, Modesto, Fresno, Stockton, etc.). And the fantasy that building housing is a path to a better economic future, without prerequisite job growth, has been totally discredited.

But never underestimate the power of a bad idea.

Affordable Housing Today

As it stands today, we really have no cohesive or financially sustainable national affordable housing programs. Federal funding assistance for affordable housing of any kind is pathetically low. Federal Low Income Housing Tax Credits only offer about $5 billion in annual assistance (Goldman Sachs will pay out almost 3 times that amount this year in executive bonuses). Section 8 vouchers only cover about 2 million households at a time when the latest census indicates that 1 in 4 families live at or below the poverty level.

Meanwhile local governments are left to fight for table scraps as state and federal government take more in taxes and fees and give back less.

Today, we have "in lieu" development where at best we get 1 or 2 so-called affordable units developed for every 8 or 9 market rate homes built (about half are for 80 percent median income, which is not all that affordable in Marin County). But the negative impacts of these projects on traffic, infrastructure, tax base, schools, the environment and everything else far outweigh their benefits.

We occasionally get some projects funded through grants, but these have been only marginally successful (e.g., the Mill Valley Fireside apartments) because the reasons for developing them are too skewed away from the reality of market economics and real demand, and tenant occupancy has reflected that.

We're told there's not enough money, that the country can't afford it. But that's only true because our spending priorities are completely out of whack (i.e. it's estimated that development of the new F-35 fighter jet will cost us $1 trillion over the next decade). In addition, the affordable housing development game is now so rigged in favor of large nonprofit developers that creative private capital is pretty much excluded. However, going forward, private capital participation will be essential.

What is Our Affordable Housing Problem?

There's no question that more federal funding would help provide financial incentives to local governments and private development interests trying to address affordable housing challenges. The trickle of funding available now is just not enough. But before we start "throwing money" at the "problem" we need to be sure what we're trying to accomplish.

Today's affordable housing challenges are very different from the real market demand for housing that followed the Great Depression and World War II. At that time, there had been no housing built in decades and there was a (baby) boom in population and household formation. Today we have just the opposite. We have a glut of housing across the country but much of it is not located where jobs are. And while traditional jobs are scarce, many newer jobs go begging because of the lack of trained candidates in the labor pool. In addition, net migration in California, for example, is currently negative: more people are moving out than moving in. Marin County has experienced stagnant population and jobs growth over the past twenty years. And ironically, the California Housing Affordability Index is at a record high. On a tax-adjusted, cash flow basis it's never been cheaper to own a home. So where's the affordable housing problem?

Our problem today is only similar to the Depression and its aftermath in that it's more about economic dysfunction and our failure to create an equitable society where real opportunity exists for all. Our problem is that while corporate profits and CEO paychecks are at historic highs, average wages, in real inflation-adjusted terms, have lagged so far behind the cost of living, and personal savings are so depleted, that even middle class people can't afford to buy a home (much less low income people). On the other hand, rents are rising because so little rental housing was built in the past two decades. So housing options are squeezed for everyone and those most in need suffer disproportionately.

It's obvious that unless we address our underlying social equity and economic problems, there will be no end to our "housing" problems. But there are still a lot of things we could be doing at a local level.

What Kinds of Housing Do We Really Need in Marin?

Quotas and mandates have clouded our thinking. Instead of counting units we should be asking what types of housing we really need. In many Marin communities, demographic trends show that we have an underserved need for many types of affordable housing that we hear little about in the media. These include:

- Housing for the elderly and assisted living facilities.
- Housing for people with disabilities and special medical needs.
- Homeless shelters and abused women's safe houses.
- Live/work opportunities like lofts and cooperative housing.
- Co-housing, where residents design and/or operate their own housing solutions (the ultimate in local control).
- Apartment building preservation, reconfiguration and substantial rehabilitation.
- Building conversions from commercial to mixed use residential.
- Sweat equity opportunities where residents can buy unfinished space to finish out themselves.
- Very small starter rental and condo units for singles and young couples.
- Smaller single family housing for the "active elderly" (partially retired and very active but not wanting any maintenance obligations).

The list is long. So let's ask ourselves, how many of these kinds of projects are we actually getting built in Marin using our present process?

The answer is none.

The Law of Unintended Consequences

One great irony is that the more laws we pass to try to force zoning changes to enable high density residential development, the more creative, mixed use / adaptive use local solutions are "crowded out" of the market. With our planning tools (zoning bonuses, density bonuses, site designation lists, fast track processing, etc.) radically skewed to support over-sized, high density in-lieu schemes, affordable housing development has become a game where those are the only projects that get considered, whether or not they make financial sense, community sense, common sense or there's any real market demand for them.

As it is, creative capital investors have little incentive to even try to fill our real housing needs (listed above) and even if we could get these kinds of projects built, most wouldn't be counted against our ABAG quota requirements.

Yet Sacramento's social engineers and ABAG planners and some of our elected representatives seem oblivious to these kinds of unintended consequences. Residents are increasingly being bullied into capitulation about quotas because they're told "it's the law." But as anyone who has actually read the prevailing mishmash of governing laws can attest, the implementation of "the law" in this case is anything but clear cut and is open to a variety of interpretations. Or at the very least there are enough gray areas to mount good arguments for local solutions and local decision making about housing needs.

But the problem is that everywhere we look we only seem to be hearing one interpretation of the law: the one that most benefits special interests that benefit from top down planning.

It's fairly obvious that Marin has many more opportunities for infill, mixed-use renovation projects with affordable units included than for "high density housing near public transportation." So why aren't we doing everything we can to help that happen instead of continuing to promote unneeded market rate, in-lieu development?

It's The Law?

As debates about local planning, General Plan updates and affordable housing heat up, it is increasingly important that the public be given the full story about what is or is not "the law." But this isn't always the case.

In Mill Valley, for example, the community has been told for years, by our Planning Department, that we are required to provide for 30 units per acre zoning: our default density for affordable housing development because we're designated an "urban" area by the State Department of Housing and Community Development (HCD). This density clearly favors large-scaled development. This was the justification for recommending approval of Planned Development (PD), high density projects on Miller Avenue, our main commercial thoroughfare.

These recommendations also came with a variety of floor area ratio (FAR) bonuses, and building setback, height and parking variances if 10 percent of the units were affordable.

This single issue about site density has been the basis of endless battles and hundreds of hours of time at public meetings. It has created enormous community ill-will and it's even driven some well-intended affordable housing developers with more modest schemes to give up and walk away. But it turns out that this isn't what state Housing Element law really requires.

The "Housing Element" is a document that the city is required to create, every 8 years, to show the state that it's making its "best efforts" to promote affordable housing in our community, by providing a list of designated sites that have appropriate zoning for development. This document is then submitted to the state for approval. Failure to file an approvable Housing Element can result in penalties from the state. However, the city is under no obligation to actually build any affordable housing. This is called an "unfunded mandate."

According to the HCD Housing Policy Development regulations on minimum densities for the Housing Element and appurtenant regulations, Mill Valley's default density is just 20 units per acre not 30. The regulations state that: "Jurisdictions (cities and/or counties) located within a Metropolitan Statistical Area (MSA) with a population of more than 2 million (Alameda, Contra Costa, Los Angeles, Marin, Orange, Riverside, San Bernardino, San Diego, San Francisco, and San Mateo) are "urban" unless a city or county has a population of less than 25,000" in which case it would be exempt from that requirement and be governed by the law's minimum, which is noted as 20 units per acre.

Residents of other communities in Marin are dealing with this kind of problem as well.

For example, op-ed pieces in the *Marin Independent Journal* regularly admonish us about our need to comply with every rule and RHNA allocation that ABAG / HCD hands us or risk onerous penalties, law suits and loss of funding.

However, as Carla Condon, councilmember from Corte Madera, has explained in great detail, this just isn't true.

No city can be denied funding for which they are otherwise eligible just because they are in a disagreement with ABAG or HCD about how to interpret their legal obligations. Again, a city is only obligated to create a Housing Element and get it certified within a specified period of time. And the kinds of "urban development" grants that are supposedly at risk have never been available to small cities in Marin anyway.

Similarly, I've read that housing renovation is not eligible to be counted toward our housing allocation quota. But again, this turns out not to be the case. Projects that qualify as "substantial rehabilitation" can qualify against ABAG housing mandates (CFR 65583(c)(1)). This kind of misinformation can discourage private capital from investing in something we actually need and can do.

Bottom line: I think the information being given to the public is grossly inadequate. In fact, getting to the truth is a full-time undertaking. ABAG has made it clear they have no intention of answering our questions. Planning "workshops" and "community input" sessions for Plan Bay Area are so tightly orchestrated that meaningful dialog is completely eliminated. And even at the local level, I've seen our hard working Planning Commissioners ask staff for clarifications about the myriad of inter-related affordable housing regulations, only to get explanations that are so simplistic, so "inside the box" that they only support the top-down point of view.

All this considered, I wonder sometimes if the fox isn't guarding the hen house, or if governing hasn't gotten so complicated that our planning officials are just in way over their heads. Either way, who is looking out for the community's interests?

In the meantime the only ones who've benefited from these one-sided interpretations of the law are ABAG and developers promoting new construction projects that are mostly market rate (i.e. highly profitable) housing.

I want to make it clear that I have nothing against profits, and there are some very good nonprofit organizations that have been building and managing affordable housing projects in Marin for decades. Many of these address real demand, like housing for the elderly and Section 8 tenants. I hope they're making a profit so they can continue to do what they do. But the widely embraced "market rate + in-lieu units" approach promoted by the ABAG quota system (which is primarily profit driven) has more downside than upside for the community and it's not going to get us where we need to go.

As it stands, by dutifully following mandates from above we're giving away the store and getting next to nothing in return.

A Cycle of Failure

Our affordable housing challenges go much further than just getting housing built. In fact, that's the easy part. In Chapter I, I talked about the demise of Pruitt Igoe as an example of a failed affordable housing concept. And there's no question that segregating the poor in isolated housing developments remains a really bad idea. But Pruitt Igoe failed for many other reasons, the most important of which was the lack of ongoing funding for maintenance, management, replacement of fixtures, appliances and equipment, and proper security.

It's easy to put up a trophy project (which Pruitt Igoe was in its day) funded by high profile, one-time grants and zoning concessions. It's easy to have a big party where self-congratulating politicians and housing advocates show up for photo ops of shovels being put into the ground. But it's a whole other thing to keep that enterprise going for the long term. It's a whole other thing to maintain the buildings year after year, and to work with families and individuals who live on the edge, day to day.

The truth is that Pruitt Igoe was abandoned by its creators and left to fend for itself as the fickle winds of politics shifted to other vote-grabbing issues, long before it was abandoned by its tenants.

We're seeing this same story unfold in Marin. A big fuss is made about the grants that help affordable projects like the Fireside in Mill Valley get built. But where will the revenues come from to keep projects like this operating and well maintained in 10 years? While housing advocates cheer on every new project proposed, regardless of its merits, the steady deterioration of our existing affordable housing stock continues to be a chronic problem. And many existing Section 8 projects around the county continue to have disproportionately higher crime rates and other ongoing management and maintenance issues that give affordable housing its bad reputation. These projects continue to need more operating funds and better management.

But where is the effort to address that need and why aren't we addressing that first?

Going forward, who will bear the social and economic burdens of future projects driven by SB375 and the *One Bay Area Plan*? And just how financially "sustainable" will the Sustainable Communities Strategy really be?

As a former affordable housing developer and owner of large Section 8 housing projects, I can say unequivocally that these types of projects are much more management and capital intensive than any other type of real estate. And when we look at the other types of affordable housing Marin communities really need or the demographic we should really be concentrating on (low and very low income residents), I don't see the sources of adequate future revenues to ensure success. But no one seems to be thinking about that right now. Affordable housing is just discussed academically, as if the world were really that simple. Right now, it's just "build baby build."

But wouldn't it make more sense to work together locally and regionally to pressure the federal government to offer better financing terms to qualified buyers (i.e. 40 year amortized mortgages) so more families could buy homes or keep the ones they have? Wouldn't it make more sense to fight for more types of financial assistance to low-income renters and landlords so renters could afford a better place to live and private property owners had more financial wherewithal to renovate and build rental housing, than to waste more precious time and money trying to re-engineer human behavior and warehouse people in high density "workforce" housing next to highways?

Making Better Decisions

One thing I'm sure of is that we're not going to solve today's planning and affordable housing challenges by continuing to rehash old ideas. More "business as usual" will just add to our long term problems. Equally, we're not going to move forward by going backwards, dismantling decades of environmental protections in the name of "streamlining" and "jobs" and "growth."

"Environmental" laws like SB375 (Chapter V) that pretend to be one thing but are driven by something else are leading to a chain reaction of bad ideas. For example, the scope of the new *"Preferred Land Use and Transportation Scenario"* just published by the TAM Executive Committee includes examining "CEQA streamlining opportunities for development projects as defined by SB375." Am I the only one whose head spins from the irony of all this?

Yes, there may be instances of abuses of environmental protection laws, but name one area of the law where that's not true. It's no justification for removing environmental review protections or not having a thorough public process.

Unfortunately, things today tend to get reduced to pointless "for" or "against" arguments. But when it comes to affordable housing, we need to be asking more substantive questions about exactly how, where, why, by what means and to whose benefit. We need to spend more time looking at unexplored alternatives. We need to move the conversation from the general to the specific. And the only way to do that is locally.

All this is the fundamental purpose of public policy.

Well-crafted local public policy has to lead our vision of the future, not consultants' opinions, not academic studies, not housing quotas, not a developer's bottom line, not special interest groups, and not some billionaire philanthropist's pet project. That's letting the tail wag the dog and only leads to knee-jerk decisions and more wasting of public assets, not lasting solutions.

The kind of process we're witnessing that substitutes orchestrated group workshops and consultants' studies for *thinking* is a recipe for disaster. I don't question for a minute the heartfelt concern and passion of affordable housing advocates for wanting to correct our world's social inequities. But I do question their understanding of economics and their acumen about the political horse-trading that's going on in Sacramento, at our expense.

But make no mistake about it, the planning challenges we're facing today are unlike anything we've dealt with in the past. The world is faster and more interdependent. Our problems are more complex and our errors will be more costly. Our environmental challenges are more precarious than ever and many affordable housing development sites that have traditionally been considered (e.g. sites at or below sea level) are no longer really viable.

We've learned so much about environmental sustainability and human health in the past 20 years, and the outcry from the scientific community is so loud and clear, that we can no longer simplistically equate "building" with "progress," or make decisions just for the sake of short-term economic growth. And we can no longer justify putting low income or elderly residents in harm's way and call it a solution.

Looking Ahead

We find ourselves in uncharted waters. The undeniable trend at the state level is the systematic dismantling of local control. Regional Housing Needs Allocations, which began decades ago as a fairly benign way of estimating growth in California in order to assist cities in planning for it, have become a heavy handed, well-funded, quota-driven system that attempts to wrest control of local planning by forcing zoning changes to accommodate high density, multi-family development (as a condition for certification of a Housing Element).

I believe this entire system needs to be questioned to its core. I remain convinced that the best affordable housing solutions will come from the local level, guided by local policy, informed by local conditions, needs and markets. There may be commonalities among the affordable housing solutions devised by different Bay Area communities and if so, that's great. But there certainly aren't any solutions that can be applied in all cases, because Marin, thank goodness, is just too nuanced for that to work.

As we look ahead toward more equitable housing solutions, in the words of Apple Computer's marketing campaign, I believe we need to "think different."

Footnotes:

[1] Green-washed laws like SB375 and proposals like the *One Bay Area Plan* are above all else about creating "jobs" in an attempt to resuscitate a real estate development and finance driven economy that will never return to its former heyday.

[2] The list of Senator Steinberg's top contributors over the years continues to be a who's who of financial, building, banking

and other real estate special interests. SB375 is a pro development, pro banking and financial services bill, wrapped in an "environmental" and "jobs creation" package. But the jobs created by development and construction are typically short-term, low quality jobs that vanish after the project is completed, and the developers and bankers have made their fees and moved on to greener pastures.

CHAPTER IV

A Criteria-Based Approach
to Housing Policy and Land Use

In response to California state requirements to create a Housing Element that addresses ABAG / RHNA housing quotas, cities in Marin have traditionally employed a "list of designated parcels" method to identify potential affordable housing sites. Lists are compiled by "planning consultants" who typically have no experience in finance or real estate development, and the results reflect their academic point of view. Employing this methodology has many inherent flaws that lead to undesirable consequences for the city, affordable housing developers and the community.

Perhaps there are better ways to address our responsibilities.

One way is by employing a "criteria-based" method of designating development sites. This approach, combined with the offering of various financial and zoning incentives, could have significant advantages over the simplistic "list the sites" approach that is presently driving so much community antagonism and distorting developers' understanding of "as of right" zoning. Since many Marin cities are now updating their General Plans and Housing Elements, I think this is a good time to consider alternatives.

At present, we compile a very limited and superficially determined list of potential housing sites that includes vacant lots, vacant buildings, aging buildings, structures on large parcels, and so forth. But due to real world circumstances many of these end up being less suitable for purchase and development than they appeared to be at first glance.

From a developer's point of view, almost all properties, developed or undeveloped, in suitably zoned residential and commercial areas are potential affordable housing or mixed use sites if the projected rental income, terms of purchase and financing are all favorable. But there is no way to determine at any given moment which properties those are, just by looking at them.

A criteria-based method designates sites for affordable housing development based on a "points" system and lets the market decide which properties have the most potential. Affordable housing developers can rely on these criteria as a guide when they analyze a property's development potential. And the proposals submitted to the city, with the highest point ratings, would qualify for the greatest number of incentives and benefits.

Possible Criteria

The "Criteria" that earn points might include a site that is:

- **_Economically obsolete_** (there is no longer any rental demand for that type of structure: i.e. a warehouse building in an office / retail area).

- **_Functionally obsolete_** (the structure is so far out of code compliance and lacks so many amenities and features that no "good" tenant will rent it).

- **_Underutilized_** (the site is far below its build out potential - allowable floor area ratio).

- **_Hazardous_** (a building that is somehow a public danger due to toxic materials, etc.).

- *Unsafe* (a structure is in danger of collapse or damage to adjacent structures, or is otherwise a public safety problem).

...and that the proposed development:

- Offers significant low and very low income units (the type and count would increase the points).

- Offers a type of housing unit that is presently desired or most needed in Mill Valley, such as live/work lofts, "starter" studio units, elderly units, etc. (Note: contrary to public perception the majority of our population is single household, single parents, elderly and renters).

- Includes desirable "green" building techniques and materials.

- Includes desirable technology and safety innovations.

- Provides a desirable public amenity (a path or lane, a public space, a shelter, parking, etc.)

- Improves public access and safety (pedestrian, vehicular, etc.).

These are just some of the possible criteria. The list needs input from planning staff, developers and the community. The actual allocation of financial and zoning incentives and/or benefits would not be automatic or purely administrative but subject to a public hearing process at the Planning Commission and City Council level.

Advantages

A criteria-based approach has many advantages. Consider the following:

1. A criteria-based method creates stated public policy objectives that developers can respond to with more certainty and creativity than a "list of designated sites" approach. This saves developers a considerable amount

of uncertainty, which is presently one of the major causes of animosity and processing difficulties.

2. A criteria-based method is responsive to dynamic and unpredictable economy and market forces, whereas a "static list" is not.

3. Under the existing "list of sites" method problems of fairness and public equity arise if a developer wants to develop a site not on the list but which is actually, based on market conditions, more easily and profitably developed.

4. We can clearly demonstrate how this criteria-based system combined with properly aligned application processing and financial incentives (tax and fee deferments or amortization, etc.) satisfies the RHNA numbers many times over.

5. This method maximizes the number of potential sites, maximizes the potential number of housing units that can be added citywide, and allows market forces and community voices to work together to achieve our goals.

6. Because this method increases the number of potential sites, it alleviates the pressure for unrealistic density.

7. The criteria-based approach could also be applied to second units and multifamily renovations - i.e. if a rehab was "significant" in that it met enough criteria to earn enough points and/or involved enough changes or upgrades, it could earn incentives. There might even be different criteria lists (variations) designed for each type of situation - i.e. new construction, renovation and second units.

Coordination

Adoption of a criteria-based approach should be carefully coordinated with the zoning code and General Plan update process.

CHAPTER V

The Truth about SB375 and the One Bay Area Plan

Throughout this book, I refer to a relatively new California State Law, Senate Bill 375 (SB375). In this Chapter, I'll delve into the details of the law and show how legislation that is promoted as "doing good" can end up doing the exact opposite.

The stated goal of SB375, which was signed into law in 2008, is "to reduce greenhouse gas emissions (GHGs) 15 percent by 2035." Its premise is that building high density development with an affordable component, close to public transportation, will decrease GHGs and thereby have a positive effect on global warming.

The rationale is as follows: Section 1(a) of SB375 states: "The transportation sector contributes over 40 percent of the greenhouse gas emissions in California. Automobiles and light trucks alone contribute almost 30 percent. The transportation sector is the single largest contributor of greenhouse gases."

This infers that SB375 will affect 40 percent of all GHG emissions in California.

To implement this law there are two basic requirements. That "prior to adopting a Sustainable Communities Strategy (SCS), the Metropolitan Planning Organization (MPO) shall quantify the reduction in GHG emissions projected to be achieved." [Section 3 (G)] and "...the MPO shall submit a description of the methodology it intends to use to estimate the

GHG emissions reduced by its Sustainable Communities Strategy." [Section 3 (I) (i)]

So I decided to analyze SB375 on its own terms to discover the truth about all this. What I discovered was that the factual basis of SB375 is faulty at best, or a carefully crafted deception at worst. In fact, SB375 will actually increase GHG emissions in California.

Falsehood #1:

"The transportation sector contributes over 40 percent of the greenhouse gas emissions in California."

The truth is that the "40 percent" figure is a 2020 projected figure, not a real measured number. The actual amount today is about 35 percent (Source: CA Air Resources Board: updated Oct. 2010). It seems to me that basing a law on a fabricated guesstimate of GHG emissions to justify the law's existence is a bit circular, isn't it?

In any case the real number, 35 percent, is also misleading because it includes emissions from airlines, trains and trams, buses, heavy construction equipment, commercial trucking and hauling, shipping, boats, ferries, etc., none of which are affected by or addressed in SB375, which only deals with housing.

Falsehood #2:

"Automobiles and light trucks alone contribute almost 30 percent."

The truth is, if you strip out the vehicles above, not affected by SB375, you're left with 23 percent of GHGs actually contributed by automobiles and light trucks. (Source: CA Air Resources Board: updated Oct. 2010).

Falsehood #3:

"The transportation sector is the single largest contributor of greenhouse gases."

The truth is, according to California EPA, energy production is the number one GHG producer in the state at 41 percent. In fact the Chevron oil refinery in Richmond, across the Bay, is the number one polluter in the San Francisco Bay Area and the entire state of California.

The entire "transportation sector" is second at 35 percent. But that includes all forms of transportation such as public transportation, trains, shipping, trucking, freight, buses, etc., none of which are covered by SB375, so it's not a helpful statistic.

But even that aside, the statistic is distorted because the California Air Resources Board's calculations err in assuming that "livestock and animal breeding" is only 3 percent, because that's just a measure of total GHG tonnage, not global warming impact. Methane gas (the majority of GHGs from livestock) is 35 times more harmful than CO^2 in its global warming impact. So livestock and breeding actually dwarfs energy and transportation combined. But not wanting to split hairs, I decided to just use the numbers we have so far.

So what are the facts?

SB375 and RHNA allocations are based on the concept that we should all carry our fair or proportional share. So I looked at the actual GHG emissions data and statistics for Marin County.

The total GHGs generated by Marin County are 2.7 million metric tons per year. With 23 percent of that from cars and light trucks, that equals 621,000 metric tons of GHG per year. (Source: Bay Area Air Quality Management District; Feb 2010 Report: Source Inventory of Bay Area Greenhouse Gas Emissions).

But 23 percent is still misleading as it relates to housing because many of our GHG emissions are not affected by SB375 or housing regardless of where we build it.

These kinds of driving needs include:

- Deliveries and pickups by car, truck and van.
- Passenger vans and shuttles to private businesses and public facilities.
- Workman and building contractors' transportation.
- Gardeners and home services.
- Utility service vehicles: water, power, sewer.
- City Agencies' vehicles: police, fire, public works.
- Health and safety vehicles.

This accounts for roughly 40 percent of vehicle use in Marin. That leaves 60 percent of 23 percent or 13.8 percent for personal travel. That equates to 372,600 metric tons GHG per year that might potentially be positively affected by SB375.

But 13.8 percent is still misleading because Marin County has no significant public transportation. According to citydata.com, 65 percent of the personal driving in Marin is driving to work. This is true regardless of where we locate housing because:

1. We cannot discriminate in rentals or sales of homes based on where people work or what kind of job they have;

2. No one can predict where they will have to go to find employment. People will go where the job is;

3. People don't make the decisions about where they work and where they live for the same reasons (i.e. you go where the best job opportunity is. You live where it's best for your family or lifestyle).

That leaves 35 percent of 13.8 percent or 4.83 percent for other personal driving, which equates to about 30,000 metric tons of GHGs per year that might potentially be positively affected by SB375.

But 4.83 percent is still misleading because most Marin County driving is not optional. The types of non-optional driving include:

- Driving to lessons, soccer, schools, friends and social activities.

- Vacations, driving to the beach or mountains, or a park, etc.

- Driving to buy large things we cannot carry (paint cans, hardware, large grocery purchases, furniture, plants, clothing, equipment, etc.).

- People shopping price not location (drive to Costco, Target, etc.).

- People having busy lives and doing multiple things in one trip so public transportation, particularly in rural Marin County, is not an option.

- People needing things not nearby (i.e. going to the doctor you need, not because he's next door).

So all in all, only about 10 percent of people, who are not doing any of these things, might be able to change their driving habits due to SB375 / One Bay Area's scheme for high density housing near the highway. That leaves only 10 percent of 4.83 percent, or 0.48 percent, which equates to 3,000 metric tons of GHGs per year could possibly be saved by SB375. And that's for the entire County of Marin!

That annual figure is approximately $1/10^{th}$ of 1 percent of all of Marin's annual GHG output. This is a statistically insignificant savings. Anything smaller than 1 percent is considered a rounding error!

But it gets worse.

SB375 / One Bay Area Will Increase GHG Emissions

It turns out that SB375 and the *One Bay Area Plan* will actually produce a dramatic increase in GHG emissions. Let's do the math.

A typical home produces about 8 tons of GHGs per year. The One Bay Area Preferred Scenario for Marin calls for the construction of 8,150 new homes. That equates to an additional 65,000 metric tons of GHGs per year.

At a development scale of 20 units per acre, about 400 acres of land developed would be required for this new housing. But I chose to use 200 acres assuming that half would be on redeveloped sites.

The annual carbon sequestration value of one acre of typical Marin undeveloped land (grass with a few trees, not forested land) is about 60 GHGs per year.

So if we lose 200 acres of land to development, that equals more than 12,000 added GHGs. If we then add the more than 65,000 tons of GHGs from the new homes, then subtract the net savings (-3,000) from SB375, we get a total added GHG emissions per year of 74,000 metric tons (77,000 minus 3,000). (Source: EPA greenhouse gas calculator).

But It Gets Even Worse

Most "affordable" units built in the future to satisfy RHNA quotas will be done using inclusionary zoning. This is true because the projects are generally not financially feasible without 80 percent of the units being sold or rented at high market rates. Inclusionary units are at best 20 percent of total units built in a project. So based on the RHNA numbers in the latest One Bay Area Preferred Scenario, we would have to build about 3 times the total number of units required by our RHNA quota, to achieve the "affordable" portion of the quota, if we use inclusionary development methods.

Doing this, will increase the total GHGs produced by SB375 by *hundreds of thousands of additional metric tons per year.*

Density Increases Greenhouse Gas Emissions

Studies show that urbanization and high density development areas in general are not just the biggest GHG producers on the planet on an overall basis but also *on a per capita basis.* New York City, for example, which would appear to be the poster child for "high density near transportation" development, is the fifth largest GHG producer on the planet.

This is not just due to the tremendous demand urbanization (and each resident per capita) puts on the environment and the regional ecosystems it impacts (that deal with its waste, sewage, and water and energy demands) but also because of a phenomenon called "heat islands." The sheer "mass" of glass, steel and concrete in urban environments eliminates the possibility of sufficient offsetting natural ecosystems to support and moderate their temperature, thereby increasing their total per capita energy demand dramatically in order to heat and cool them year round.

So high density living, at least using our present construction methods, may appear efficient in the short term but that isn't the same as being environmentally beneficial in the long term, particularly when you include the external demands it places on regional ecosystems. Cities with the highest densities import more water and power from greater distances (with greater losses and costs along the way) and export more GHGs because they cannot be mitigated locally.

Marin, on the other hand, with its livable scale and balance of developed land to open space, produces less overall environmental impact and mitigates much of its GHG output locally. Certainly there's more we must do but Marin may already be the best model of sustainability found anywhere in this country.

Wasting Taxpayer's Time and Money

Again, the basic premise of SB375 is that we need to build high density affordable housing near transportation to achieve GHG reductions. However, this also assumes that building these units will somehow make economic sense. But let's look at how that "pencils."

The cost of building a 20 unit project in Marin today, using the inclusionary affordable housing method, is about $15 million dollars ($3 million for land; $12 million for hard and soft building costs). But maybe we get lucky so let's say it costs $12,500,000. Using the typical inclusionary affordable housing formula, that would produce 4 affordable units (20 percent of the units) which would cost $625,000 per unit ($12,500,000 divided by 20 equals $625,000 each).

But what we really need to know is the "public cost" of developing the affordable units.

Calculating the "public cost" of the development of the affordable units would have to include valuing the cost to taxpayers for federal rent subsidies, reduced interest rate loans, allocations of Low Income Housing Tax Credits, the gifted value of land and development rights that developers receive from the cities or counties or through state density bonuses, and the loss of real estate taxes due to affordable housing development's exemption. We need to factor in the value of waived or reduced local permitting and processing fees and other incentives and off-setting costs. And we need to assess the burdens this development puts on existing infrastructure, schools and public services, and the time and cost incurred by cities and communities in holding public hearings and workshops and other such application processing requirements. On top of this we also have to factor in a percentage of the enormous taxpayer expense of operating the quasi-public oversight agencies that are driving all this (ABAG, BAAMQ,

MTC, etc.), which costs taxpayers well over one hundred million dollars every year.

All of this adds to the total public cost per unit of affordable housing.

Of course, the public cost per affordable unit will vary from location to location and is dependent on the specifics of each development proposal. But for simplicity, let's be conservative and say that the total gifted value of all the public costs noted above for a new 20 unit development, with inclusionary affordable housing units, represents a 10 percent reduction in the overall development cost. That would result in a total public (taxpayer) cost of approximately $1,388,900 in public subsidy (the total discounted development cost of $12,500,000 equals 90 percent of the total development cost: $13,888,900; 10 percent equals $1,388,900). For the sake of simplicity, let's just round that down to $1,380,000. So the taxpayer subsidy that is required to build 4 affordable housing units results in a subsidized public cost of approximately $345,000 per unit.

Now let's assume that the families in those four affordable units owned 6 cars (1.5 cars per family) and that those cars get average gas mileage and produce typical GHG emissions. But driving a Prius, compared to the average car, cuts GHG emissions by about 60 percent right now, instead of the 15 percent goal of SB375 in twenty years. And a new Toyota Prius costs about $25,000.

So if we bought each new affordable unit family new Prius's (instead of building them a unit that cost the public $345,000 to develop), doing the math, we could give these four families 6 new Priuses for $150,000 (1.5 cars per household multiplied by 6 equals $150,000) and come out with approximately four times less GHG emissions than the goals of SB375 - not by 2035 but today – and save the public $1,230,000 (4 units at $345,000 per unit in public subsidy equals $1,380,000, minus $150,000 equals $1,230,000)!

Heck, why not buy all 20 families Priuses? That would cost $750,000 (30 cars) and really do something to decrease GHGs, and we'd still save taxpayers $630,000! And after all, $750,000 is just "expense account" money for big agencies like ABAG and MTC, every year.

The point of this exercise is to show that we can solve the problem we set out to solve - to lower GHG emissions dramatically – right now, without any development at all. Or at the very least, we can allow growth to happen organically and be managed locally by changing the vehicles we own, and in the process achieve more public benefit with less waste of taxpayer funds and less environmental destruction. So I ask you, which is the better investment of public funds and the public's time?

Solutions?

The problem today is that cars and light trucks produce GHG emissions. So why not just fix the problem instead of destroying our communities, and creating unsustainable growth and unwieldy bureaucracies that are only adding to the problem?

We should force vehicle manufacturers to produce more fuel efficient cars, trucks and other transportation right now. One simple way would be to levy an MPG tax on every new car or truck sold that doesn't get at least 35 miles per gallon (the newly proposed 2016 Corporate Average Fuel Economy -

CAFE standard) then offer a corresponding tax credit for the purchase of any new cars or trucks that exceed it. This would penalize low miles per gallon / high pollution vehicle manufacturers and reward high miles per gallon / low pollution vehicle manufacturers. It would make high mpg vehicles cheaper for consumers to purchase, by comparison, increasing sales of the kinds of vehicles we want people to drive.

Now add trade-in rebate programs for very old vehicles still on the road and similar point of sale taxes and tax credits for zero-emissions vehicles (electric, natural gas, hydrogen fuel cell, biofuels, etc.) and reward innovation. [1]

None of this would cost consumers or taxpayers anything. This approach would decouple personal transportation from city planning in a way that would no longer be as dysfunctional as it is under SB375, and it would allow growth and development to once again respond to real local needs. And the free market would ensure that innovation in non-polluting car and truck design advanced rapidly, as manufacturers competed for consumer dollars.

It's time to penalize the source of GHGs and pollution, not taxpayers and everyday citizens who are pushing back on over-reaching central planners, trying to save the communities they've worked so hard to create.

SB375 & One Bay Area

SB375 and One Bay Area are an ideological approach without any statistical or scientific basis. Their "top down" housing mandates and compliance demands are unprecedented in California legal history and remove significant local control of zoning and planning. Building housing without first creating jobs leads to "unsustainable" development (think: Vallejo, Modesto, Stockton and Fresno). SB375 and One Bay Area are economically destabilizing and financially irresponsible. They are environmentally destructive and contradict the fundamental laws of supply and demand, free markets, and how cities grow and survive.

I believe that SB375's legal ambiguities and contradictions make it open to legal challenge as to the enforceability of some of its more onerous provisions.

What is most troubling is that in the end, after all the costs and burdens that SB375 and One Bay Area will impose on our communities, it will not result in providing what we really want: more high quality jobs and more quality, affordable housing choices to those most in need.

Footnotes:

[1] In 1948 an engineer at Studebaker modified a straight six engine with a single barrel carburetor to get 78 miles per gallon. The new plug-in Prius (originally invented by a guy in Larkspur, California, in his garage) gets about 88 miles per gallon. General Motors sued the state of California to stop our attempts to increase mileage standards, for 20 years... right up to the day they declared bankruptcy (and were bailed out by you know who). The means to double vehicle gas mileage has been readily available for a long time.

The Truth about SB375 and the One Bay Area Plan

CHAPTER VI

Public Policy, Community Voices & Social Equity

Black Tuesday; the Crash of 1929 - Library of Congress

"Toto, I don't think we're in Kansas anymore."
~ The Wizard of Oz

Since the market crash of 2008, real estate developers, financiers and politicians have been in panic mode. Though it's clear that the debt fueled hyper-growth of past decades is gone forever, they remain in deep denial. Like some neurotic gambler who's lost it all but who's still hitting the tables believing he can get it all back, these powerful interests continue to roll the dice, regardless of the social and community costs (quality of life, infrastructure, traffic, schools, etc.), regardless of the environmental costs, and regardless of the destabilizing economic impacts in the long run. The tragedy of all this is how much damage could be done trying to bring back the "good old days."

The concentration of wealth and power at the top and the influences of special interests are distorting everything in our country including local planning priorities. As I've tried to illuminate, we can't continue to pursue top down central planning practices or social engineering experiments that have repeatedly failed in the past. And since "the market" has not solved all our problems as promised, and left too many needs unmet, what should we be doing?

I have no intention of wrapping this all up with a simplistic "to do" list. I only hope this book can act as a catalyst for more productive dialog. Solutions can only start in each community, each in their own way. But one thing that is clear is if we want to bring about effective change, our city and county officials are going to have to step outside their historical comfort zones of only looking at issues that are strictly local. We can no longer divorce ourselves from the big picture because it's what is increasingly driving everything.

It's true that in Marin County most city council members are unpaid volunteers and legitimately complain about having too big a workload as it is. So it's hard enough to get them to cooperate on Marin's shared concerns much less problems that have state, national or international implications. But then again, planning staff is generally very well paid and could be doing much more.

Isolationism has worked in the past but we just don't live in that world anymore.

What Is the Problem We're Trying to Solve?

Marin's fundamental disconnect with the ABAG / MTC / One Bay Area / New Urbanism approach is that the planning challenges in Marin today are in many ways the opposite of what the One Bay Area approach was created to address. As I've said in Chapter I, we already have much of what it promises in terms of sustainability and quality of life. And Marin's affordable housing needs are quite different from most of the other ABAG communities.

In more urban parts of the Bay Area (San Francisco, Oakland, Emeryville, San Jose, etc.) market rate, single family residential homes are more difficult to build profitably and average household incomes are lower, but there are more opportunities to find high density housing sites. So in those cities it makes some sense to promote market rate housing development in addition to inclusionary affordable units. But in Marin the only thing developers want to build is single family, detached, market rate housing or high end condos so, we shouldn't have "quotas" for that (or quotas at all for that matter).

Our problem is that there is little we can do to incentivize developers to build low and very low income housing and the other types of housing we really need. But Marin's challenges are about more than just the size or distribution of RNHA allocation numbers.

Housing Elements and Land Entitlement

When Marin cities draft their Housing Elements, they typically include a list of designated sites for rezoning for affordable housing. In the past this has been a relatively benign exercise and generally considered an "unfunded mandate."

But that has changed.

As I've discussed in Chapter IV, creating a specific list of sites has actually never been a good idea. It arbitrarily skews property valuations and essentially gives entitlement advantages to one property owner over another for no good reason other than one site might be vacant land. It's inequitable and offers no incentive for property owners who are not on the list to step up and propose affordable housing or mixed use projects. These are some of the reasons why the criteria-based method I proposed, led by public policy, would be better for all concerned.

However, even with that aside, in our new regulatory climate the creation of a fixed "list of sites" is now more problematic than before.

Senate Bill 375 has created a link between zoning and the Housing Element sites list. It adds language that creates a legal gray area that could allow a private developer to force a zoning change to high density residential, if their proposed project qualifies by having at least 49 percent affordable units. Now a newly proposed bill, SB226, would remove California Environmental Quality Act (CEQA) protections for "infill" development (a vaguely defined term), and the Transportation Authority of Marin's (TAM) recent *"Preferred Land Use and Transportation Scenario"* proposes that transit-oriented development sites be entirely exempt from CEQA review. Finally, SB1220 (see Chapter II, pg. 25) contemplates a state controlled fund to finance these kinds of projects.

In combination, these laws effectively strip away our Conditional Use and Planned Development (PD) zoning approval protections and eliminate CEQA Environmental Impact Reports, leaving only our Design Review process, which is not adequate and in many cases would no longer be a legal method to stop projects we don't want.

This legal nexus between the Housing Element (part of the General Plan) and SB375 essentially means that putting a site on a list has now become a significant step toward land rights entitlement (financial value) that developers can rely upon. And developers can sue to protect these entitlements even though they may not even own the property yet (it can be under option to purchase), and the city has not yet rezoned it.

We should not underestimate the formidable challenges to local control these regulations could bring about once there is sufficient funding to aggressively enforce them.

Affordable Housing Demand

There is no question that affordable options in Marin are scarcer than in some other parts of the region. But the existence of high-priced suburban communities like those found in Marin is true in every metropolitan area in the country. *It's the price we pay for a free society.* So this fact of life, in and of itself, is neither discriminatory nor justification for running roughshod over local zoning control.

In addition, often quoted statistics about how many people work in Marin and live elsewhere are not the same as proof of "market demand" for housing. If that were the case, the Fireside Project in Mill Valley would have filled up in 10 minutes instead of 2 years and the Millworks project in Novato would not have resulted in huge financial losses. I wonder how much more "progress" our communities will have to endure before housing advocates accept this truth.

These projects founder because they ignore how markets work. Housing construction cannot logically precede economic growth or jobs growth because the quality of that growth and the kinds of jobs created determine what kinds of housing are needed, not vice versa.

The only real evidence we have of affordable housing demand remains the County's Section 8 waiting list (something we should be addressing much more effectively). Other arguments about housing our police officers, firefighters and government workers ring hollow. Today, government workers on average make more than comparable private sector employees (salary, benefits, retirement and health care). And just ask a firefighter or policeman about where he or she lives.

Our "workforce" clearly understands the difference between what they will do to get a job and where they want to live with their families. Given the choice of living in a cramped apartment "project" or driving an hour and renting (or owning) a single family home with a yard, it's no contest what they will choose every time.

So who exactly are we trying to help?

Social Engineering at Its Worst

I recently had the opportunity to sit in on a Town Council meeting in Corte Madera where Mark Luce, president of ABAG, made a presentation defending the value of being an ABAG member city. His boilerplate presentation was unsurprising in that it had only good things to say about the agency and its goals. His "facts" were typically one-sided and his conclusions about the greenhouse gas emissions consequences of SB375 were academic and inaccurate (Chapter V). But what was most striking was when he began to espouse the virtues of social engineering.

Mr. Luce made it clear that he believes it's socially equitable to provide high density housing next to freeways for our low income "workforce." But he went on to say that this kind of housing was good for "these people" because if they worked near their apartment (I assume in a low paying service job) they would spend more time with their children, inferring that they would therefore be better parents.

Astonishingly, he felt ABAG somehow had the moral authority to pass this kind of judgment on other people's parenting. But what was even more amazing was how surprised and clueless he was when people on the Council and in the audience reacted in shock to his over-reaching and high-handed remarks.

He finally admitted that this was perhaps only his opinion but he seemed to have no qualms about enforcing it on others, even though he holds no elected office with the powers to do so (nor does anyone else, thankfully).

I'm sure Mr. Luce would be the first one to be aghast if I told him that he had to move his family from the comfort of their bucolic Napa Valley home to live in an apartment in Corte Madera next to a highway on-ramp. Yet he saw no incongruity at all in his ringing endorsement of "engineering" that outcome for "our workforce."

Workforce Housing

Well-intended housing advocates (who are unwittingly carrying water for development interests in Sacramento) often try to characterize local resistance to affordable housing as a "civil rights" issue or the result of "racism" (in addition to the NIMBY argument noted in Chapter III) [1]. But it seems to me that it's the RHNA quota system, dutifully enforced by subservient ABAG planners, that is promulgating racist or certainly "classist" thinking about the needs of "those people" who will live in their beloved high density projects.

In fact I think the entire concept of "workforce housing" is elitist. "Our workforce" is discussed as if working people are second class citizens who don't need yards for their children to play in, fresh air to breathe, views of something other than a concrete off-ramp, or God forbid to be paid a living wage in the first place. Well, this may come as news to those who sit in high positions at ABAG, MTC, BCDC and BAAQMD, and Sacramento politicians and affordable housing advocates, but "those people" who live in low income housing have the same hopes and dreams for their family and their children's future that you do. They only live there because they have no other choice.

They are not "our workforce." They are our fellow citizens, entitled to want the same things we enjoy, regardless of their financial status, education, ethnicity or lack of luck in life.

We're often told that too many workers have to come from Richmond, across the Bay, to work in Marin and that this is the reason we need to invest in more affordable housing. But the more obvious question is why aren't we, as a society, investing in education, jobs and community development in Richmond so people can find high paying work there and have a safe community to live in? Then maybe people in Marin would have to start paying their imported housekeepers, nannies and gardeners a decent living wage and benefits to compete.

Sometimes I wonder whose lifestyle we're really trying to improve.

But then, even when we do offer low income residents a chance to buy a home here, we deny them the only real value of home ownership: equity appreciation. We cap the upside in affordable units with appreciation profit deed restrictions for 30 or 40 years, and deny them the fruits of sweat equity. This is nothing more than a modern version of indentured servitude.

I think the whole thing is absolutely shameful.

The "Market"

What affordable housing advocates forget is that it wasn't the massive projects the government built that ultimately solved the housing shortages of the late 1940's and 1950's. Like it or not, it was the much maligned, privately financed developments like Levittown, incentivized by the G.I. Bill and federally insured mortgages, that filled the need.

That said, I'm not suggesting that markets will solve all our problems or that we should build more Levittowns, quite the opposite. Without government support at all levels, the market will remain incapable of providing housing for those most in need (low and very low income residents). But what I am suggesting is that private investment, backed by strong policy incentives, can help provide a great deal of the kinds of housing we really need. The blunt instrument of massive quasi-government agencies (ABAG, MTC, et al) getting involved in local zoning and planning won't. The *One Bay Area Plan* approach micro-manages everything to death.

Finally, we can't afford to keep sending tax money up to the federal and state level only to have it come back in the form of policies that remove control over local decision making and work against our community planning interests. Likewise, waiting for real change to come from the top is pointless.

So where does that leave us?

Show Me the Money

Everywhere we look today we're told there's no money to pay for anything we need. "Austerity" is the big buzzword. And discussions about the role of government have distilled down to "less government" versus "more government." This makes long term planning more difficult. But the problem is not whether we need more government or less government. It's how to get "better" government and more efficient and productive government for "less" cost. And in the process we have to create more "value" from what we do.

Our national public policy and financial challenges are far too numerous and complex to address in this book. However, there are a few things we need to understand to make better decisions locally.

The historic lows in interest rates being paid by the U.S. government have a lesson to teach us. At a time when we are "lending" our government money in unprecedented amounts for a negative return (inflation adjusted), the market is telling us that it's not a lack of money that's the problem. It's the lack of confidence that anything is worth taking the risk to invest in.

We need to think about how to break this logjam.

Under the circumstances, I would suggest that it's the federal government's responsibility to "invest" that money back into the country, and local government's responsibility to make our needs known to them. It may seem counter-intuitive but when money is almost free and everyone is paralyzed by fear, it's a good time to borrow and invest for the long term.

But in our post "debt bubble" world, our money must be spent more wisely.

Nuts and Bolts and Finance

I think the "bailout" of General Motors has been tarred unfairly. I think it was a smart move. With GM, rather than being the "banker" of last resort, the U.S. Treasury acted as the "investment banker" of last resort and the result so far has been profitable for U.S. taxpayers. The funds GM received were not a gift but an investment in return for an equity stake. Could this be a way to finance planning and housing initiatives?

Grants, bonds and tax incentives will undoubtedly continue to play an important role in affordable housing finance and housing markets in general. And I would argue for the need to expand Section 8 subsidies with new types of vouchers that offer more local control over how they are used. But providing local, state and federal government-backed financing, debt insurance and even equity participation to the mix may be the better way to move ahead than traditional government "hand-outs." New types of public / private partnerships could also increase financial leverage and provide a backstop for innovative local solutions.

For example, Napa County has a small equity-sharing program that offers interest free funds that buyers can use toward their down payment when they purchase a home. Repayment is due on sale. It helps people who otherwise couldn't qualify. This kind of incentive could also be accomplished by insuring mortgage debt in exchange for equity. And programs like these scale up well from humble beginnings.

It may take years for housing markets to fully recover and we may see flat home prices with little inflation adjusted appreciation for a decade, but it's time to plan for the future.

Affordable Housing and Social Equity

There was a saying in the 1960's: "If you're not part of the solution, you're part of the problem." The updated version of that should be: "If you don't see that it's all connected, you don't understand the problem." Social equity is a complex challenge.

Ensuring a quality education, including college, for everyone who's willing to work hard to earn it is essential for our society's long term success. But saddling the next generation with $100,000 in debt before they even get their first job is no way to promote household formation or social equity (this is a perfect example of how we've passed the costs of our economic failures onto the next generation). And where will their jobs come from unless we support the kinds of industries we'll need to live in a sustainable world?

Local zoning and planning can play a special role here, nurturing new, sustainable businesses like green technology and medical research.

We know that investing in our health pays back many times over in increased productivity, lower medical costs, and greater happiness. And happy, productive people have families, buy homes and strengthen communities. But almost 20 percent of our population has no healthcare coverage and even people with health insurance are just one major illness away from bankruptcy. And with hunger becoming a widespread problem, how can we expect anyone to escape poverty if they have to worry about getting enough to eat every day? Yet local stores and restaurants throw out enough food every week to feed thousands.

Finally, issues like Marin County pension reform and social equity are connected simply because our financial resources have limits. Yet we have our county supervisors dolling out taxpayer-funded "discretionary grants" to questionable pet projects and political allies, while allowing vital health services like the County Public Health Lab in San Rafael to close down. The annual expenditures of our county supervisor's personal slush funds (which are unique in all of California) greatly exceed the cost of running the San Rafael lab. Yet not a single supervisor has offered to give back those funds to save it.

Social equity is also about getting our priorities straight.

Public Transportation and Growth

We hear a lot of talk from ABAG and MTC about public transportation and building high density housing near "quality" transportation corridors (an oxymoron in Marin, if there ever was one). But here's my question: how did we get to this place where everything is backwards?

Historically, public transportation was built to serve economic growth and population demand, not to create it. Railroads connected distant regions to facilitate commerce. Subways and trolleys allowed people to get around more efficiently in crowded cities. But now we have transportation planners dictating where growth is "supposed to" happen and how we should engineer it.

Thankfully, our cities are already very "walkable." Still, it's true that Marin's population would be better served by more public transportation options. As it stands, Marin has no significant public transportation other than bus routes. With the topography, street configurations and geographical distances between cities in Marin being what they are, other kinds of public transportation that work in urban areas (subways, light rail, etc.) just won't work here. And any public transportation system that's going to work in Marin is going to have to be extremely flexible, adaptive and non-polluting.

But there are possibilities.

For example, one solution might be a fleet of relatively inexpensive electrically powered shuttle buses monitored and managed in real time by a wireless "demand" sensing system; 21st century street cars (as opposed to SMART trains – Sonoma-Marin Area Rail Transit – that are costing us $650 million and counting).

Each shuttle would travel on a "flexible" route that can adapt to rider demand. Riders with registered accounts or pre-paid trip cards can "tell" the system that they need a pickup at a shuttle stop by inserting their card in a reader or notifying the system via a smartphone app. The shuttle bus routes and stop locations are predetermined but shuttle drivers know beforehand whether or not there are riders there in need of pickups. So the system offers feedback to adapt the diver's route to operate at maximum efficiency. The route configurations can also "learn" from experience and adapt to changes in user demand, over time.

Or perhaps we should be promoting car-sharing (like Zipcars), using hybrid or electric vehicles, to alleviate traffic congestion and promote a healthful environment.

The point is there are many things we can do locally that are relatively inexpensive (and possibly even profitable) and can be implemented quickly. We need to consider all our public transportation options rather than confine ourselves to the traditional thinking proposed by ABAG, MTC and the One Bay Area approach.

Local Voices Equal Better Solutions

Marin's unique housing and planning challenges are a strong argument for a Marin Council of Governments (COG). Corte Madera has proposed that a Marin COG or a North Bay COG that includes Marin, Napa and Sonoma, would have many advantages. For one thing a Marin COG would allow us to develop our own criteria for our Sustainable Communities Strategy (SCS) and our own Housing Needs Analysis. These would be based on our own job and population growth projections and our unique community assets, not a generic formula foisted on us by Sacramento.

Working together, we would have the critical mass to deal with the state directly regarding our Regional Housing Needs Allocations (RHNA) and more effectively argue for the types of housing we really need.

The "party line" response to this idea is that a Marin COG is bad because we'd just end up fighting amongst ourselves, city against city, about how to divide up our RHNA allocations instead of fighting with ABAG. Wow, talk about cynicism! With that attitude and that complete lack of faith in the judgment, intelligence, creativity and motivations of our neighboring cities, no wonder there's so little cooperation or innovation at the top. Seeing challenges like this as opportunities instead of obstacles is called "leadership." It's the fundamental ability required to be an effective public servant. And I think anyone who espouses this simple-minded objection has given up on democracy and should be voted out of office.

But there is another reason to have a seat at the table in Sacramento via our own COG. It involves our ability to lobby for or against some of the regulations that are headed our way. Having a Marin COG that promotes an agenda that serves our communities, rather than development and financial special interests, could be an important step toward shaping how new laws like SB375, and potentially SB226 and SB1220, are administered.

A Marin COG could support the kinds of solutions that are best adapted to our local needs.

Leadership and New Directions

So where will leadership come from? In addition to forming a Marin or North Bay COG, I think the Marin County Council of Mayors & Council Members is a good place to start. This sleepy organization could quickly reinvent itself as a force for collaboration and change. They already have the platform to hold countywide forums on major issues, do countywide assessments of public opinion, and study alternatives.

They only need to act.

Another interesting approach would be the creation of a hybrid nonprofit / for profit "venture philanthropy fund" that focuses on financing local planning and affordable housing initiatives.

As it is now, on one side we have traditional stand-alone nonprofit foundations that often have agendas that are not necessarily aligned with the goals of Marin cities. And on the other side we have for profit investors and nonprofit housing developers that find it hard to make the numbers work to build the kinds of projects Marin really needs or to incorporate our big picture planning goals into their plans.

In the middle are small Marin cities that lack sufficient funding for full time staff dedicated to project finance. So, housing and planning decisions end up being made through a mish-mash of competing financial interests or available grants, which rarely results in positive community outcomes.

A hybrid venture fund might offer a way to help facilitate better solutions and have advantages over traditional philanthropy or housing trusts. It can potentially attract more money because it can work on countywide initiatives that have a larger scope and a longer time horizon, and it can source funds from both donors and investors. With a hybrid fund, for profit corporations and individual investors collaborate side by side with foundations, individual donors, donor advised funds, non-governmental organizations (NGOs) and local and state government, with each receiving the kinds of investment returns or public benefit outcomes they require.

This financing model is being used successfully at the film finance nonprofit organization that I currently manage and extensively by others for medical research and technology development.

With a hybrid entity, every type of financing option is available and investment sources need not be local. For profit investors can retain equity, provide loans, participate in revenues, and use return-enhancing financial leverage. Nonprofit participants can provide grants, low cost loans, loan guarantees, and participate in financial upside through the use of program related investments. And local governments can participate through the issuance of bonds or participation certificates.

All these methods can be brought together a single initiative or spread across a wide variety of projects.

A venture philanthropy fund could also work closely with a Marin COG and individual Marin cities to analyze and finance planning and housing solutions. And its involvement could include promoting Marin's funding opportunities to the national investment and donor community, and lobbying for Marin's financial interests in Sacramento. This kind of hybrid funding approach might be particularly applicable for financing privately owned infill, second unit, building conversion, renovation, and mixed use development. The kind of development that is scattered throughout the cities on small parcels is not the kind built by major developers, but is the most desirable and best suited for our "built out" Marin cities.

Another challenge Marin cities face is that the majority properties with development or re-development potential are owned by individual property owners who are risk adverse and not development minded. No amount of policy changes or incentives will convince these owners, who are principally interested in the tax benefits and revenues their rents generate, to take on financial risks and become speculative "developers" or full time property managers. A venture fund could offer these owners joint venture partnership arrangements and could help cities structure financial instruments that could offer these property owners ways to mitigate development risk and bring in professional management when projects are completed.

A comprehensive discussion of this is beyond the scope of this book. But it's an intriguing idea.

Working Collaboratively

I want to thank all those throughout Marin, in and out of government, who have challenged conventional wisdom and spoken out for local control and sustainable growth in spite of considerable pressure and criticism. And I want to thank all the long-time community activists who've fought lonely battles for decades to preserve our environment and demand better government.

However, far too many people still continue to live in their own little worlds, falling back on the excuse that they are just too busy to get involved. But if you don't participate, if you don't make your voice heard, you will get what you deserve. What worries me, though, is that if you don't speak up, I may also get what you deserve. So I would ask everyone to please join in. Those leading the call for new approaches and greater government transparency need your support. I encourage everyone whose community is facing the kinds of challenges discussed in this book to write letters, send emails, attend meetings, meet with your elected representatives and make some noise, so you'll be heard over the relentless din of special interests. If we want sustainable solutions, that's where it all starts. As they say, "Democracy is not a spectator sport."

Marin cities, like all other small cities in diverse regions across the nation, need to work together on housing, planning and social equity challenges, while change is still possible and local control still exists. This is an instance where self-interest and common interest are one in the same.

We need to get ABAG and Sacramento to understand that the unique characteristics of our communities are our strengths that can inform unique locally-driven solutions rather than obstacles to their simple-minded goals from the top.

Hard Truths

At the beginning of this book I talked about company towns like Pullman, Illinois. We look back at those times as a Gilded Age of robber barons and hard times. But the sad truth is that what we do today in terms of helping low income workers doesn't come close to measuring up.

Employment at Pullman was a sought after and prestigious position. The single family homes offered to employees were a big step up from what the average family lived in at the time, and it came with family health care, clean streets, good schools and a safe neighborhood. Likewise, Henry Ford offered his workers the highest average pay of any company in the country so they could afford to buy his cars, without concern that his stock would lose value or he'd lose his year-end bonus.

Today, corporations sell us planned obsolescence, bankroll protective legislation and bankrupt themselves to avoid pension obligations, while worker pay and benefits plummet. Meanwhile, young billionaire CEOs and hedge fund traders congratulate themselves on their brilliance, forgetting the century of hard work that laid down the infrastructure of a society that made their insignificant moment in the sun possible.

Historically, we've always defined "solutions" in terms of economic solutions. But as we approach the limits to our growth (at least under our current methods), our attention will need to turn to other qualifiers like the environment and quality of life. It's a conversation we've never really had to have before.

It would be a mistake to characterize our challenges as a simple Republicans versus Democrats or liberal versus conservative story. It's much more than that. Our predicament is the result of an unchecked public and private sector that's been steadily falling deeper and deeper into debt for decades. It's about waging wars we can't afford and accumulating mountains of fanciful "stuff" on credit that we can't afford to pay off. It's about inefficiencies everywhere we look and shoveling money into "wasting assets" instead of making long term investments. And as a result, we find ourselves unable to do the things we really need to do. But that doesn't diminish our need to do them.

Today we find ourselves besieged from all sides by special interests trying to deconstruct decades of environmental protections and much needed social safety net programs. And it's all in the name of "jobs" or "processing efficiency" or "boosting the economy" or some other short term fix. But it's just more of the same thing that got us where we are and it won't work.

I wonder why it's so hard for us to do the right thing for the long run. Is shortsightedness programmed into our hunter-gatherer brains? Yes, providing affordable housing opportunities and achieving greater social equity will probably mean higher progressive taxes. But few remember that in the 1950's, the much romanticized decade that built the backbone of our economy, marginal tax rates on high earners approached 90 percent.

So if you make a lot of money and you have to pay higher taxes, why not just be grateful that your parents and grandparents did the heavy lifting that made it easier for you to become as wealthy as you are? Social equity and sustainable solutions will require sacrifices.

I think it will be worth it.

Footnotes:

[1] It is a common misconception that Covenants, Conditions and Restrictions (CC&Rs) with racial and religious restrictions are somehow historically unique for Marin and therefore of special significance. The unfortunate truth is that these types of provisions were once, more often than not, included in almost every type of subdivision and land sales CC&Rs, and many times even in local building codes across the country. Some of those precluded from ownership or membership or even visitation, that I've seen over the years around the country, have included Blacks, Hispanics, Asians, Jews, Catholics, Irish and Italians, to name a few. These provisions became unenforceable after the civil rights laws passed in the 60's.

Epilogue

The Big Con

How an 1868 Iowa state court ruling led to
unfunded, pro-development housing mandates in Marin.

Justice James Forrest Dillon – 1868
Library of Congress

The California State Constitution requires the state to reimburse local governments for state mandates. "Unfunded mandates," which are orders that induce "responsibility, action, procedure or anything else that is imposed by constitutional, administrative, executive, or judicial action" for state and local governments and/or the private sector, are not allowed.

If this is true, how did we end up in a situation where the State of California is sucking more and more of our tax dollars up to Sacramento while making more and more demands on local county and city governments about educational requirements, health and safety requirements, and particularly on local planning requirements and things like affordable housing Regional Housing Need Allocation (RHNA) quotas, without providing any funding to accomplish them? And if they don't provide funding, how are they able to force us spend so much of our local time and money to comply with them, holding public hearings, doing expensive studies, creating Housing Elements, and crafting elaborate 20 year plans?

I'm not a lawyer but it seems to me these are questions someone should be asking. And as the financial situation for California cities and counties becomes increasingly dire and more and more cities declare bankruptcy due to lack of funding, why aren't any of our elected officials asking these questions?

So I decided to do some digging. And in my research, I kept coming across something called "Dillon's Rule."

Dillon's Rule

According to *Black's Law Dictionary*, Sixth Edition, *Dillon's Rule* is a rule handed down from an 1868 Iowa State Court case that has been used ever since in interpreting statutes delegating authority from states to local government. In the case of *Clinton v Cedar Rapids and Missouri River Railroad* (24 Iowa 455; 1868), Justice John Forrest Dillon ruled that "Municipal corporations owe their origin to and derive their powers and rights wholly from the legislature." In plain English this meant that cities and counties only have the powers that are expressly granted to them by their states. Without the state's granting of powers, cities and counties have no inherent powers themselves.

Apparently, since then this ruling has become the cornerstone of an endless number of court decisions regarding the rights and powers of cities and counties.

To understand why this ruling came about, a little history is helpful. In 1868, shortly after the Civil War ended in 1865, the country was not anything like it is today. States, or what was left of many of them, had very weak governments while many local jurisdictions (cities and counties) were by and large run like private fiefdoms that were notoriously financially corrupt. And many cities and county governments didn't accept (have never accepted?) that the war was over. They pretty much made up their own laws which varied widely from one place in the state to the next.

So in order to bring about some semblance of order to our newly re-formed "Union" the courts took the position that's stated in Dillon's Rule. Strictly interpreted it meant that a city had to ask the state for permission to levy a tax or create a new ordinance. In those times, this probably made good sense. Today, when states hold all the power and cities and counties are weak and without significant resources or options, it makes no sense at all.

The effect of Dillon's Rule and its legal interpretation is still subject to great debate. However, as time passed, many states adopted "Home Rule" laws that freed up the situation a bit (California being one of them). Home Rule essentially said that cities and counties could pass their own laws and taxes (without asking permission) so long as those laws and taxes didn't contradict state law.

Okay, so far I understood all this, at least in theory. But you're probably asking what this all has to do with unfunded mandates?

There's No Free Lunch

As I've pointed out before, starting in the early 1990's the "spend more than you earn," debt and leverage game in our state and federal government and in our economy started in earnest. The federal government began to amass enormous public debt and states quickly followed close behind, piling on one unfunded liability after another. As a result, California started down the road of withholding more and more taxes and fees from cities and counties while at the same time dramatically expanding the number of state mandated programs and standards required of those cities and counties.

But wait a minute, didn't that directly contradict the California State Constitutional prohibition against unfunded mandates? Well, yes, it did. But in order to allow them to continue to pass legislation that they didn't have to pay for, the California State Legislature pulled off an act of "spin" worthy of Machiavelli. They cited an interpretation of Dillon's Rule that said that local governments are "administrative arms of the states and can be ordered to carry out state programs or policies generally referred to as mandates."

Huh? Did you get that? In other words the state legislature turned the original intention of Dillon's Rule on its head. In layman's language they said that what Dillon's Rule really meant was that the state *can require* unfunded mandates if they *decide to* (i.e. they legislate it to be so) because cities and counties only derive their powers from the state. And since "home rule" says that cities and counties can only have powers over things that are not precluded by the state legislature then voila!, unfunded mandates are fine so long as the legislature *legislates* them to be so.

In know. I'm still scratching my head, too. But subsequent legal challenges, particularly regarding school funding issues, have largely failed to correct this. This opened the floodgates to the avalanche of unfunded mandates that have been cascading out of Sacramento ever since, having dramatic impacts on our schools, infrastructure, public services and yes, affordable housing and local planning. This brings me to the current situation in Marin regarding ABAG's affordable housing, quota driven, One Bay Area, Transit Oriented Development / Sustainable Communities Strategy / Preferred Scenario, etc., etc., mess at hand - all of which adds up to one huge unfunded mandate.

So what have our elected representatives been doing about all this? With all the resources and bright legal minds at their disposal (courtesy of our tax payments) isn't there any reasonable argument that can be brought forward to challenge this? Isn't it time someone stepped up and questioned whether or not it's appropriate to allow the California State Legislature to cite a one hundred and forty four year old court ruling as a basis to contradict the clear intentions of our state Constitution, prohibiting unfunded mandates?

Needless to say, all this bothered me to no end. How could this be happening? And then it hit me. It's no longer about doing what's right or wrong, or financially prudent, or good for taxpayers in Sacramento. It's really all about what is politically easiest.

The Big Schmooze

Think of it this way: You're an elected official or political appointee, sitting in your office in Sacramento, worrying about the things that are most important to you like getting re-elected or re-appointed, increasing your power and political influence, enjoying the fabulous perks of your position (free health care, great retirement benefits, etc.), and most importantly increasing the number of financial supporters contributing to your campaign fund. And with all this important stuff to worry about you're faced with a choice. Do I roll up my sleeves and try to really fix this financial mess we call California (or the United States for that matter) and take on pension reform, government inefficiency, tax reform, affordable housing, education, etc., etc.? Or do I just keep passing "responsible sounding" legislation (e.g. SB375) that only ends up adding to the long list of unfunded mandates and costly responsibilities of cities and counties downstream?

Hmmm… which is easier politically and less controversial with my friends and colleagues here in Sacramento? How can I appear "do the right thing" policy-wise (good sound bites in the media) but not add to the state's budget deficit (to show how "responsible" I am)? And most of all, which choice will allow me to continue to "go along to get along" and move up the political food chain?

It's pretty clear the choice they've been making. And locally we now live in a world where everything we thought, for decades, we were paying taxes for, like running our schools and fixing our roads and keeping our parks open, we now have to pay for by voting to tax ourselves *again* with new sales and income taxes, special bonds and fees and assessments.

The Big Spin

In the 1960's a small group of Marin residents, calling themselves the Golden Gate Headlands Committee, took on the Marin County Supervisors and fought against all odds to save the Marin Headlands, a movement that led to the creation of the Golden Gate National Recreation Area which became the cornerstone of everything we enjoy and prize about Marin. Millions of people come from around the world every year to cross the Golden Gate Bridge and take picture perfect photos of the San Francisco skyline from its lofty hillsides.

These preservationist pioneers were not "important" people in high places. They we just regular citizens who saw the truth of things and stood up for it. And they were ruthlessly ridiculed as radicals, hippies, no-growth fanatics, NIMBY's, communists and worse.

Today local elected officials and self-appointed "leaders" of housing advocacy groups shamelessly wrap themselves in the memory of those early environmental visionaries to promote massive social engineering policies and misguided, pro-development legislation in support of the MTC / ABAG / *One Bay Area Plan* juggernaut. And at the same time they label the groundswell of local community voices now rising against it as radicals, no-growth fanatics, NIMBY's, and worse, apparently without the slightest awareness of the irony of it.

Coda

My question is where does this all end? When are we going to find the political will to say no to ill-conceived, financially burdensome, community destroying, unfunded mandates and begin to really plan for a truly sustainable Marin with the kinds of services and development and affordable housing we really need?

Regrettably, however, I doubt we'll see any evidence of that until the number of community voices reaches a tipping point where elected officials, political appointees, and paid planning staff begin to worry about their jobs.

Sources:

- *Federal and State Mandating on Local Governments: Report to the National Science Foundation*; Catherine H. Lovell, Max Neiman, Robert Kneisel, Adam Rose, and Charles Tobin, Riverside, CA: University of California, June 1979.

- *The Regional Governing of Metropolitan America*; David Y. Miller; Westview Press, 2002.

- *Dillon's Rule is From Mars, Home Rule is From Venus: Local Government Autonomy and the Rules of Statutory Construction;* Jesse J. Richardson, Jr. Virginia Tech, 2005.

- *GG32 - Reform the State Mandates Process to Make Reimbursement More Cost-Efficient, Predictable and Fair*; CA.Gov: California Performance Review; 2012.

- *California Legislative Unfunded Mandates and Realignment Impacts on Local Governments;* Allen K. Settle, Ph.D. Professor, California Polytechnic State University, San Luis Obispo, California; March 22-24, 2012.

FINAL THOUGHTS

Growth, Planning and Climate Change

Some people have commented to me that we have no choice but to accept the Smart Growth / *One Bay Area* vision of our future, being promoted by regional planners, because the urgency of our climate change crisis demands that we do everything we can, right now, without hesitation. But doing "everything we can" and doing "more of the same" is an important distinction we need to make.

There are a couple things wrong with the argument that says we have to take action indiscriminately. The first is the assumption that there is an egalitarian "we" that can respond effectively to climate change issues. Our country just doesn't work that way, except when power hungry government agencies or multi-national corporations go unchecked. We remain a "republic" where sovereignty is vested in the individual, and so public consensus is required to effect real change. The second flaw is the assumption that One Bay Area is a viable solution based on the premise that high density development reduces greenhouse gases (GHG). As I've discussed in Chapter V, this is a fallacy.

The truth is that while individuals are offered very few real GHG reducing options in the basic services and products we need to buy, the real GHG culprits, energy producers, corporate agribusiness, transportations manufacturers, consumer products manufacturers and heavy industry, continue to resist changes to their business-as-usual methods.

Years of professionally managed messaging and green-washed advertising have "shamed" people into obsessing about every drop of water they waste, every table scrap that's not composted and every slip of paper not recycled. This brainwashing is happily promoted by mainstream media looking for a "story," and by large corporations and government agencies looking to increase their reach. But it averts attention from the real story. As a result, many educated, well-intended, socially conscious people are convinced that everything is their responsibility and the future will be bleak without immediately adopting "solutions" like One Bay Area.

This is pure nonsense.

Climate change solutions need to first and foremost address the sources of greenhouse gases "up the ladder" before forcing burdensome adaptations on individuals and small communities "down the ladder." Our climate change problems are primarily a national policy failure which is expressed through dysfunctional tax, subsidy and funding mechanisms. Our federal government has never had a national energy policy and still refuses to cooperate with every other industrialized nation in the world on climate change treaties. This has to change and it has to change soon before too much of our planet's regenerative capabilities are lost.

Taxpayers in the U.S. spend almost a trillion dollars a year subsidizing oil and gas (tax subsidies, program subsidies etc.), while new energy technologies and products wither and die due to lack of financial support. We're told that we can't afford to do what's good for the environment because it will cause people to lose their jobs. Meanwhile, all the jobs that have been created by emergent, green technologies, most of which we invented here in the United States, have gone overseas to Asia and Europe. We're in danger of turning into an economy built on high frequency trading, iPhone apps and burger flipping. I wonder what it will take to wake us up.

I find it ironic that while we talk incessantly about being "competitive" in our personal pursuits and sports and business and in the world economy, everything we proudly refer to as human "progress" has been a triumph of "collaboration" over competition. The rule of law, fair markets and democracy are all collaborative innovations. They're all based on the premise that it's better to have cooperative ground rules, even if it means not always getting our own way, than it is to only be out for ourselves and constantly battling with each other over everything. So how many more forests need to be lost, or fisheries and coral reefs decimated, or species gone extinct before we understand that the "tragedies of the commons" do, in fact, affect us all? How many toxic chemicals do we need to spew into our air and dump into our water supply before we realize that we're not just poisoning our world but ourselves?

My point is that global environmental challenges are the most important issues of our time and none of them will be addressed by New Urbanism, Smart Growth or more high density housing near public transportation. It's just more of the same old, same old, with a new marketing pitch. In fact, all current science would suggest that we should dramatically slow down development and growth, and learn to all live with less, until we find ways to do it in a sustainable way. If we really believe we owe the next generation any semblance of the kind of world we enjoyed, we have to take a hard look at ourselves and the way we plan for the future.

No reasonable person is arguing against any growth at all. Certainly, mixed-use and infill housing and higher density in appropriate settings (as decided on a community by community basis) are possible, perhaps even desirable. But the next time you hear someone telling you to dutifully resign yourself to a bleak future vision like One Bay Area, I urge you to stand up to the fashionable thinking of our times and just say "No."

We need to nurture local voices and lead with innovation and community participation, not give up all we have worked so hard, for generations, to create. The vicious cycle of endless growth, urbanization and false hopes pinned on delusional social engineering and central planning have always failed and will always fail.

The new world of shared information, brought on by the Internet, has deconstructed every human endeavor, from banking to shopping to scientific research and education. "Planning" remains one of the few remaining archaic, top down, enterprises left standing.

That is about to change.

APPENDIX A

We Don't Want "One Bay Area"

The following is the text of an Op-Ed piece which challenges the fundamental concept of the One Bay Area Plan. Published 3/29/12.

These are uncertain times. But if there's one thing I'm sure of, it's that no one decides to live in the San Francisco Bay Area because it's "One Bay Area."

If anything, we're the poster child (and the butt of endless jokes) for diversity of people, ideas and "place."

But lately, however, we're inundated with guilt-giving Op-Ed pieces extolling the virtues of central planning and a dystopian vision called the *One Bay Area Plan*. It's wrapped in politically correct phrases like "affordable housing" and "reducing greenhouse gases" and comprised of a truckload of contradictory laws, terms and agencies like SB375, AB32, RHNA, ABAG, MTC, TAM, BCDC, BAAQMD, PDAs, SCSs and APDs - enough to take a thousand lawyers a thousand years to comprehend.

This "nexus of nonsense" is the work of prominent politicians, backed by deep pocket development and construction interests, "ladder climbing" staff and local elected officials, and a non-stop chorus of shaming from brown-nosing, wannabe bloggers and agenda-driven, nonprofit academics, funded by anti-local control social engineers.

The only problem with this cacophony of "smart" growth advocacy is its complete lack of common sense and factual basis.

We're told we can "build our way out of climate change" (SB375), which, even disregarding for a moment its complete lack of scientific basis, defies even a 6th grader's sense of logic. We're told that "housing is the key to sustainability," though all evidence points to the exact opposite.

Truth be told, housing has nothing to do with sustainability, economic, environmental or otherwise. Las Vegas, Denver and Atlanta all bore the worst of the housing bust because they overbuilt their real housing needs. Manhattan and San Francisco have never had enough affordable housing yet they thrive. The South Bronx and Oakland have always had an excess of affordable housing and they continue to struggle. From the Sumerians to the Mayans, the real cause of unsustainability has been resource depletion from too much growth, as will be the case with water in Marin.

And who's to say it wouldn't be better for the planet to build entirely new "green" towns hundreds of miles north of Marin County, where a balance of development and impacts could be better achieved? I don't know, but I do know it's not Sacramento central planners who should decide.

But then why let facts get in the way of a good jobs program in an election year?

Still, even as ABAG pressures us to build, we've always had the comfort of believing that as an unfunded mandate, very little development was actually going to happen. However, now we have SB1220, brought to us by some of the same people who brought us SB375 (Darrel Steinberg). It proposes a $75 tax on recording any document related to real estate transactions and the $1 billion a year in proceeds into a bureaucratic black hole called the "Housing Opportunity Trust," in Sacramento. Decisions about how the money is spent will now be governed only by political agendas and big money special interests.

SB1220, combined with SB375's plan to "warehouse" the poor in high-density developments next to highways and rename open space "resource areas," may represent the final nail in the coffin of local control of zoning and property rights. Generations of effort to create Marin's unique quality of life will be dismantled. The same financial interests that bankrupted private capital markets worldwide and got bailed out with tax payer money (big banking and financiers) are now intent on doing the same thing to our "public capital" markets, our tax dollars.

We cannot afford to let this happen.

And in the end, my bet is that One Bay Area's stillborn vision of homogenization still won't have solved the core problem: providing quality housing choices for those most in need.

APPENDIX B

An Alternative Analysis to the Development of Miller Avenue in Mill Valley

This is a link to a privately funded study that was presented to the Mill Valley City Council in October of 2007, but its principles apply to all cities.

This information is provided for those wanting an example of more in-depth financial analysis that supports the land use proposals put forth in Chapter IV: A Criteria-Based Approach to Housing Policy and Land Use.

Read the Alternative Analysis Study at:

http://www.friendsofmillvalley.org/files/MillerAvenuePlanAna lysisv10.pdf